BREAD

igloobooks

igloobooks

Published in 2014
by Igloo Books Ltd
Cottage Farm
Sywell
NN6 0BJ
www.igloobooks.com

Food photography and recipe development: PhotoCuisine UK
Front and back cover images © PhotoCuisine UK

FIR003 0714
2 4 6 8 10 9 7 5 3 1
ISBN 978-1-78343-463-3

Printed and manufactured in China

Contents

Classic Loaves

Crusty White Bloomer

Makes: 1 | Preparation time: 2 hours | Cooking time: 40 minutes

---

Ingredients

**400 g / 14 oz / 2 ⅔ cups strong
white bread flour, plus
extra for dusting**

½ tsp easy-blend dried yeast

1 tbsp caster (superfine) sugar

1 tsp fine sea salt

1 tbsp olive oil

Method

Measure all of the ingredients into the bread machine with 280 ml / 9 fl. oz / 1 cup of water and set it to the 'dough only' setting.

When the dough is ready, turn it out onto a lightly floured work surface. Shape the dough into an oval bloomer and transfer to a greased baking tray, then cover with oiled cling film and leave to prove for 1 hour or until doubled in size.

Preheat the oven to 220°C (200°C fan) / 425F / gas 7.

Dust the loaf with flour and slash the top with a sharp knife. Transfer the tray to the top shelf of the oven.

Bake for 40 minutes or until the loaf sounds hollow when you tap it underneath. Transfer to a wire rack and leave to cool completely before serving.

100%
Wholemeal Loaf

Makes: 1 | Preparation time: 2 hours | Cooking time: 40 minutes

Method

Measure all of the ingredients into the bread machine with 280 ml / 9 fl. oz / 1 cup of water and set it to the 'dough only' setting using the 'wholemeal' option if available.

When the dough is ready, turn it out onto a lightly floured work surface. Press it out into a rectangle, then roll it up tightly and transfer to a greased baking tray. Cover with oiled cling film and leave to prove for 1 hour or until doubled in size.

Preheat the oven to 220°C (200°C fan) / 425F / gas 7.

Dust the loaf with flour. Transfer the tray to the top shelf of the oven.

Bake for 40 minutes or until the loaf sounds hollow when you tap it underneath. Transfer to a wire rack and leave to cool completely before serving.

Ingredients

400 g / 14 oz / 2 ⅔ cups stoneground wholemeal flour, plus extra for dusting

½ tsp easy-blend dried yeast

1 tbsp caster (superfine) sugar

1 tsp fine sea salt

1 tbsp olive oil

Small Cob Loaves

Makes: 2 | Preparation time: 2 hours | Cooking time: 25–30 minutes

Ingredients

400 g / 14 oz / 2 ⅔ cups strong white bread flour, plus extra for dusting

½ tsp easy-blend dried yeast

1 tbsp caster (superfine) sugar

1 tsp fine sea salt

1 tbsp olive oil

Method

Measure all of the ingredients into the bread machine with 280 ml / 9 fl. oz / 1 cup of water and set it to the 'dough only' setting.

When the dough is ready, turn it out onto a lightly floured work surface, split it in half and shape into two round loaves.

Transfer the cobs to a greased baking tray and cover with oiled cling film. Leave to prove for 1 hour or until doubled in size.

Meanwhile, preheat the oven to 220°C (200°C fan) / 425F / gas 7.

Dust the cobs with flour and slash a cross in the tops with a knife. Transfer the tray to the top shelf of the oven.

Bake for 25–30 minutes or until the loaves sound hollow when you tap them underneath.

Transfer to a wire rack and leave to cool.

Muesli Rolls

Makes: 12 | Preparation time: 2 hours | Cooking time: 15–20 minutes

Method

Measure all of the ingredients into the bread machine with 280 ml / 9 fl. oz / 1 cup of water and set it to the 'dough only' setting.

When the dough is ready, turn it out onto a lightly floured work surface, split it into 12 even pieces and shape into rolls. Transfer the rolls to a greased baking tray and cover with oiled cling film. Leave to prove for 1 hour or until doubled in size.

Preheat the oven to 220⁰C (200⁰C fan) / 430F / gas 7.

Dust the rolls with flour and slash the tops with a knife. Transfer the tray to the top shelf of the oven.

Bake for 15–20 minutes or until the rolls sound hollow when you tap them underneath. Transfer to a wire rack and leave to cool.

Ingredients

350 g / 12 ½ oz / 2 ⅓ cups strong white bread flour, plus extra for dusting

50 g / 1 ¾ oz / ⅓ cup stoneground wholemeal flour

75 g / 2 ½ oz / ¾ cup muesli

½ tsp easy-blend dried yeast

1 tbsp caster (superfine) sugar

1 tsp fine sea salt

1 tbsp olive oil

Granary, Wheat and Rye Bread

Makes: 1 loaf | Preparation time: 2 hours | Cooking time: 35–40 minutes

Ingredients

200 g / 7 oz / 1 ⅓ cups stoneground wholemeal flour

100 g / 3 ½ oz / ⅔ cup rye flour

100 g / 3 ½ oz / ⅔ cup granary bread flour

1 tsp easy-blend dried yeast

1 tbsp caster (superfine) sugar

1 tsp fine sea salt

1 tbsp olive oil

Method

Measure all of the ingredients into the bread machine with 280 ml / 9 fl. oz / 1 cup of water and set it to the 'dough only' setting, using the 'wholemeal' option if available.

When the dough is ready, turn it out onto a lightly floured work surface and shape it into a round loaf. Transfer the loaf to a greased baking tray and cover with oiled cling film. Leave to prove for 1 hour or until doubled in size.

Meanwhile, preheat the oven to 220⁰C (200⁰C fan) / 430F / gas 7.

When the dough has risen, transfer the tray to the top shelf of the oven.

Bake for 35–40 minutes or until the loaf sounds hollow when tapped. Transfer the bread to a wire rack and leave to cool.

Walnut and Rye Bread

Makes: 1 loaf | Preparation time: 2 hours | Cooking time: 35–40 minutes

Method

Measure all of the ingredients into the bread machine with 280 ml / 9 fl. oz / 1 cup of water and set it to the 'dough only' setting.

When the dough is ready, turn it out onto a lightly floured work surface and shape it into a long loaf. Transfer the loaf to a greased baking tray and cover again with oiled cling film. Leave to prove for 1 hour or until doubled in size.

Meanwhile, preheat the oven to 220⁰C (200⁰C fan) / 430F / gas 7.

When the dough has risen, slash along the length of the loaf with a sharp knife.

Transfer the tray to the top shelf of the oven.

Bake for 35–40 minutes or until the loaf sounds hollow when tapped. Transfer the bread to a wire rack and leave to cool.

Ingredients

200 g / 7 oz / 1 ⅓ cups strong white bread flour, plus extra for dusting

200 g / 7 oz / 1 ⅓ cups rye flour

1 tsp easy-blend dried yeast

1 tbsp caster (superfine) sugar

100 g / 3 ½ oz / ¾ cup walnuts, chopped

1 tsp fine sea salt

1 tbsp walnut oil

Multigrain Bread

Makes: 1 loaf | Preparation time: 2 hours | Cooking time: 35–40 minutes

Ingredients

200 g / 7 oz / 1 ⅓ cups strong white bread flour, plus extra for dusting

200 g / 7 oz / 1 ⅓ cups malted granary flour

½ tsp easy-blend dried yeast

1 tbsp caster (superfine) sugar

1 tsp fine sea salt

100 g / 3 ½ oz / 1 cup rolled porridge oats

55 g / 2 oz / ½ cup golden linseeds

55 g / 2 oz / ½ cup hemp seeds

1 tbsp sunflower oil

Method

Measure all of the ingredients into the bread machine with 280 ml / 9 fl. oz / 1 cup of water and set it to the 'dough only' setting.

When the dough is ready, turn it out onto a lightly floured work surface and shape it into a loaf.

Transfer the loaf to a greased baking tray and cover again with oiled cling film. Leave to prove for 1 hour or until doubled in size.

Meanwhile, preheat the oven to 220°C (200°C fan) / 425F / gas 7.

When the dough has risen, slash the top with a sharp knife.

Transfer the tray to the top shelf of the oven.

Bake for 35–40 minutes or until the loaf sounds hollow when tapped.

50-50 Rye Batons

Makes: 2 | Preparation time: 2 hours | Cooking time: 30 minutes

Method

Measure all of the ingredients into the bread machine with 280 ml / 9 fl. oz / 1 cup of water and set it to the 'dough only' setting.

When the dough is ready, turn it out onto a lightly floured work surface then divide it into two pieces and shape into fat batons. Transfer the batons to a greased baking tray and cover with oiled cling film. Leave to prove for 1 hour or until doubled in size.

Meanwhile, preheat the oven to 220°C (200°C fan) / 425F / gas 7.

Slash a diamond pattern across the top of each baton with a sharp knife. Transfer the tray to the top shelf of the oven.

Bake for 30 minutes or until the loaves sound hollow when you tap them underneath. Transfer to a wire rack and leave to cool completely.

Ingredients

200 g / 7 oz / 1 ⅓ cups strong white bread flour

200 g / 7 oz / 1 ⅓ cups rye flour

½ tsp easy-blend dried yeast

2 tbsp caster (superfine) sugar

1 tsp fine sea salt

1 tbsp olive oil

Crusty Cobble Loaf

Makes: 1 | Preparation time: 2 hours | Cooking time: 40 minutes

Ingredients

400 g / 14 oz / 2 ⅔ cups strong white bread flour, plus extra for dusting

½ tsp easy-blend dried yeast

1 tbsp caster (superfine) sugar

1 tsp fine sea salt

2 tbsp olive oil

Method

Measure all of the ingredients into the bread machine with 280 ml / 9 fl. oz / 1 cup of water and set it to the 'dough only' setting.

When the dough is ready, turn it out onto a lightly floured work surface. Shape the dough into a square loaf and transfer to a greased baking tray, then cover with oiled cling film and leave to prove for 1 hour or until doubled in size.

Preheat the oven to 220°C (200°C fan) / 425F / gas 7.

Transfer the tray to the top shelf of the oven.

Bake for 40 minutes or until the loaf sounds hollow when you tap it underneath. Transfer to a wire rack and leave to cool completely before serving.

Spelt Loaf

Makes: 1 loaf | Preparation time: 2 hours | Cooking time: 35–40 minutes

---

Method

Measure all of the ingredients into the bread machine with 280 ml / 9 fl. oz / 1 cup of water and set it to the 'dough only' setting.

When the dough is ready, turn it out onto a lightly floured work surface and roll it into a fat sausage. Turn it 90⁰ and roll it tightly the other way, then tuck the ends under and transfer the dough to a loaf tin. Cover the tin loosely with oiled cling film and leave to prove somewhere warm for 1 hour.

Preheat the oven to 220⁰C (200⁰C fan) / 430F / gas 7 and dust the top of the loaf with flour.

Bake for 35–40 minutes or until the loaf sounds hollow when you tap it underneath. Transfer the bread to a wire rack and leave to cool completely.

Ingredients

200 g / 7 oz / 1 ⅓ cups white spelt flour, plus extra for dusting

200 g / 7 oz / 1 ⅓ cups wholemeal spelt flour

1 tsp easy-blend dried yeast

1 tbsp caster (superfine) sugar

1 tsp fine sea salt

1 tbsp olive oil

Crusty Bread and Rolls

Makes: 1 loaf and 6 rolls | Preparation time: 2 hours | Cooking time: 25–35 minutes

Ingredients

**350 g / 12 ½ oz / 2 ⅓ cups
strong white bread flour, plus
extra for dusting**

**50 g / 1 ¾ oz / ⅓ cup
stoneground wholemeal flour**

½ tsp easy-blend dried yeast

1 tbsp caster (superfine) sugar

1 tsp fine sea salt

1 tbsp olive oil

Method

Measure all of the ingredients into the bread machine with 280 ml / 9 fl. oz / 1 cup of water and set it to the 'dough only' setting.

When the dough is ready, divide in half and shape one half into a loaf and the other into six rolls. Transfer to a greased baking tray and cover with oiled cling film. Leave to prove for 1 hour or until doubled in size.

Preheat the oven to 220°C (200°C fan) / 430F / gas 7.

Dust with flour and slash the tops with a knife. Transfer the tray to the top shelf of the oven.

Bake for 15–20 minutes or until the rolls sound hollow when tapped underneath. Cook the loaf for a further 10–15 minutes. Transfer to a wire rack and leave to cool.

Rye Bread

Makes: 1 loaf | Preparation time: 2 hours | Cooking time: 35–40 minutes

Method

Measure all of the ingredients into the bread machine with 280 ml / 9 fl. oz / 1 cup of water and set it to the 'dough only' setting.

When the dough is ready, turn it out onto a lightly floured work surface and shape it into a round loaf. Transfer the loaf to a greased baking tray and cover with oiled cling film. Leave to prove for 1 hour or until doubled in size.

Meanwhile, preheat the oven to 220⁰C (200⁰C fan) / 430F / gas 7.

When the dough has risen, score the top with a knife and dust with flour. Transfer the tray to the top shelf of the oven.

Bake for 35–40 minutes or until the loaf sounds hollow when tapped. Transfer the bread to a wire rack and leave to cool.

Ingredients

400 g / 14 oz / 2 ⅔ cups rye flour, plus extra for dusting

1 tsp easy-blend dried yeast

1 tbsp treacle

1 tbsp malt extract

1 tsp fine sea salt

1 tbsp olive oil

Mouna

Makes: 1 | Preparation time: 3 hours 30 minutes | Cooking time: 30 minutes

Ingredients

250 g / 9 oz / 1 ¼ cups butter, cubed

400 g / 14 oz / 2 ⅔ cups strong white bread flour

2 ½ tsp easy-blend dried yeast

4 tbsp caster (superfine) sugar

1 tsp fine sea salt

4 large eggs, plus 3 egg yolks

3 tbsp sugar nibs

Method

Measure all of the ingredients except for the sugar nibs into the bread machine and set it to the 'dough only' setting, using the 'enriched' option if available.

When the dough is ready, scrape it into a lined shallow round cake tin, then cover with oiled cling film and leave to prove for 2 hours or until doubled in size.

Meanwhile, preheat the oven to 220°C (200°C fan) / 425F / gas 7. Slash a star in the top with a sharp knife and sprinkle with sugar nibs.

Bake the mouna for 10 minutes, then reduce the heat to 190°C (170°C fan) / 375F / gas 5 and bake for a further 20 minutes or until the underneath sounds hollow when tapped. Turn the mouna out onto a wire rack and leave to cool completely before serving.

Ciabatta Pavés

Makes: 4 | Preparation time: 2 hours | Cooking time: 15 minutes

Method

Measure all of the ingredients into the bread machine with 200 ml / 7 fl. oz / 1 cup of water and set it to the 'dough only' setting.

When the dough is ready, turn it out onto a lightly floured work surface. Press it out into a square, then cut it into quarters.

Transfer the four pieces to an oiled baking tray, cover with oiled cling film and leave to prove for 1 hour or until doubled in size.

Meanwhile, preheat the oven to 220°C (200°C fan) / 425F / gas 7.

Bake for 15 minutes or until the underneaths sounds hollow when you tap them. Transfer the loaves to a wire rack and leave to cool completely.

Ingredients

100 g / 3 ½ oz / ⅔ cup strong white bread flour

200 g / 7 oz / 1 ⅓ cups of pasta flour, plus extra for dusting

½ tsp easy-blend dried yeast

1 tsp fine sea salt

2 tbsp olive oil

Kamut Bread

Makes: 1 | Preparation time: 2 hours | Cooking time: 40 minutes

Ingredients

400 g / 14 oz / 2 ⅔ cups kamut flour, plus extra for dusting

½ tsp easy-blend dried yeast

1 tbsp caster (superfine) sugar

1 tsp fine sea salt

1 tbsp olive oil

Method

Measure all of the ingredients into the bread machine with 280 ml / 9 fl. oz / 1 cup of water and set it to the 'dough only' setting.

When the dough is ready, turn it out onto a lightly floured work surface. Shape the dough into a round cob loaf and transfer to a greased baking tray, then cover with oiled cling film and leave to prove for 1 hour or until doubled in size.

Preheat the oven to 220°C (200°C fan) / 425F / gas 7.

Dust the loaf with flour and cut a cross in the top with a sharp knife. Transfer the tray to the top shelf of the oven.

Bake for 40 minutes or until the loaf sounds hollow when you tap it underneath. Transfer to a wire rack and leave to cool completely before serving.

Seed and Grain Loaf

Makes: 1 loaf | Preparation time: 2 hours | Cooking time: 35–40 minutes

Method

Measure all of the ingredients into the bread machine with 280 ml / 9 fl. oz / 1 cup of water and set it to the 'dough only' setting.

When the dough is ready, turn it out onto a lightly floured work surface and shape it into a loaf.

Transfer the loaf to a greased baking tray and cover with oiled cling film. Leave to prove for 1 hour or until doubled in size.

Meanwhile, preheat the oven to 220°C (200°C fan) / 425F / gas 7.

When the dough has risen, slash the top with a sharp knife.

Transfer the tray to the top shelf of the oven.

Bake for 35–40 minutes or until the loaf sounds hollow when tapped.

Ingredients

200 g / 7 oz / 1 ⅓ cups strong white bread flour, plus extra for dusting

200 g / 7 oz / 1 ⅓ cups malted granary flour

½ tsp easy-blend dried yeast

1 tbsp caster (superfine) sugar

1 tsp fine sea salt

100 g / 3 ½ oz / 1 cup rolled porridge oats

55 g / 2 oz / ½ cup golden linseeds

55 g / 2 oz / ½ cup hemp seeds

1 tbsp sunflower oil

Tuscan Saltless Batons

Makes: 2 | Preparation time: 2 hours | Cooking time: 30 minutes

Ingredients

400 g / 14 oz / 2 ⅔ cups strong white bread flour

½ tsp easy-blend dried yeast

2 tbsp olive oil

Method

Measure all of the ingredients into the bread machine with 280 ml / 9 fl. oz / 1 cup of water and set it to the 'dough only' setting.

When the dough is ready, turn it out onto a lightly floured work surface then divide it into two pieces and shape into fat batons. Transfer the batons to a greased baking tray and cover with oiled cling film. Leave to prove for 1 hour or until doubled in size.

Meanwhile, preheat the oven to 220°C (200°C fan) / 425F / gas 7.

Slash the top of each baton with a sharp knife. Transfer the tray to the top shelf of the oven.

Bake for 30 minutes or until the loaves sound hollow when you tap them underneath. Transfer to a wire rack and leave to cool completely.

Sesame Rolls

Makes: 12 | Preparation time: 2 hours 30 minutes | Cooking time: 15 minutes

Method

Measure all of the ingredients except for the sesame seeds into the bread machine with 280 ml / 9 fl. oz / 1 cup of water and set it to the 'dough only' setting.

When the dough is ready, turn it out onto a lightly floured work surface. Shape the dough into 12 rolls and transfer to a greased baking tray, then cover with oiled cling film and leave to prove for 1 hour or until doubled in size.

Preheat the oven to 220°C (200°C fan) / 425F / gas 7.

Slash a cross into the top of each roll with a sharp knife and sprinkle with sesame seeds. Transfer the tray to the top shelf of the oven.

Bake for 15 minutes or until the rolls sound hollow when you tap them underneath. Transfer to a wire rack and leave to cool completely before serving.

Ingredients

400 g / 14 oz / 2 ⅔ cups strong white bread flour, plus extra for dusting

½ tsp easy-blend dried yeast

1 tbsp caster (superfine) sugar

1 tsp fine sea salt

1 tbsp sesame oil

3 tbsp sesame seeds

Walnut Brioche Loaf

Makes: 1 | Preparation time: 3 hours 30 minutes | Cooking time: 30 minutes

Ingredients

250 g / 9 oz / 1 ¼ cups butter, cubed

400 g / 14 oz / 2 ⅔ cups strong white bread flour

2 ½ tsp easy-blend dried yeast

4 tbsp caster (superfine) sugar

1 tsp fine sea salt

4 large eggs, plus 3 egg yolks

100 g / 3 ½ oz / ¾ cup walnuts, chopped

Method

Measure all of the ingredients into the bread machine and set it to the 'dough only' setting, using the 'enriched' option if available.

When the dough is ready, scrape it into a lined loaf tin, then cover with oiled cling film and leave to prove for 2 hours or until doubled in size.

Meanwhile, preheat the oven to 220°C (200°C fan) / 425F / gas 7.

Bake the brioche for 10 minutes, then reduce the heat to 190°C (170°C fan) / 375F / gas 5 and bake for a further 20 minutes or until the underneath sounds hollow when tapped. Turn the brioche out onto a wire rack and leave to cool completely before serving.

Ciabatta

Makes: 1 | Preparation time: 2 hours | Cooking time: 20 minutes

Method

Measure all of the ingredients into the bread machine with 280 ml / 9 fl. oz / 1 cup of water and set it to the 'dough only' setting.

When the dough is ready, turn it out onto a lightly floured work surface. Use two plastic scrapers to fold the top and bottom of the dough into the middle, then repeat with the sides. Flour the work surface next to the ciabatta with flour and roll the dough onto it, then dust the top with flour and transfer to a baking tray.

Cover with oiled cling film and leave to prove for 1 hour or until doubled in size.

Meanwhile, preheat the oven to 220°C (200°C fan) / 425F / gas 7.

Bake for 20 minutes or until the underneath sounds hollow when you tap it. Transfer the loaf to a wire rack and leave to cool completely.

Ingredients

100 g / 3 ½ oz / ⅔ cup strong white bread flour

200 g / 7 oz / 1 ⅓ cups of pasta flour, plus extra for dusting

½ tsp easy-blend dried yeast

1 tsp fine sea salt

2 tbsp olive oil

Gluten-free Batons

Makes: 3 | Preparation time: 2 hours | Cooking time: 30 minutes

Ingredients

400 g / 14 oz / 2 ⅔ cups gluten-free bread flour

1 tsp easy-blend dried yeast

1 tbsp caster (superfine) sugar

1 tsp fine sea salt

1 tbsp olive oil

Method

Measure all of the ingredients into the bread machine with 280 ml / 9 fl. oz / 1 cup of water and set it to the 'dough only' setting, using the 'gluten-free' option if available.

When the dough is ready, turn it out onto a lightly floured work surface then divide it into three pieces and shape into long batons. Transfer the batons to a greased baking tray and cover with oiled cling film. Leave to prove for 1 hour or until doubled in size.

Meanwhile, preheat the oven to 220°C (200°C fan) / 425F / gas 7.

Make a slash along the length of each baton with a sharp knife. Transfer the tray to the top shelf of the oven.

Bake for 30 minutes or until the loaves sound hollow when you tap them underneath. Transfer to a wire rack and leave to cool completely.

Savoury Breads

Gruyère Loaf

Makes: 1 loaf | Preparation time: 2 hours | Cooking time: 35 minutes

Ingredients

100 g / 3 ½ oz / 1 cup Gruyère, grated

400 g / 14 oz / 2 ⅔ cups strong white bread flour, plus extra for dusting

½ tsp easy-blend dried yeast

1 tsp fine sea salt

1 tbsp olive oil

Method

Measure half of the cheese into the bread machine with the rest of the ingredients and 280 ml / 9 fl. oz / 1 cup of water, then set it to the 'dough only' setting.

When the dough is ready, turn it out onto a lightly floured work surface and press it out into a rectangle. Roll it up tightly and transfer to a lined loaf tin. Cover with oiled cling film and leave to prove for 1 hour or until doubled in size.

Preheat the oven to 220°C (200°C fan) / 425F / gas 7 and sprinkle the rest of the cheese over the loaf.

Bake for 35 minutes or until the loaf sounds hollow when you tap it underneath. Transfer to a wire rack and leave to cool completely before serving.

Wholemeal Tomato Bread

Makes: 1 loaf | Preparation time: 2 hours | Cooking time: 35–40 minutes

Method

Measure all of the ingredients, reserving 3 tomatoes, into the bread machine with 280 ml / 9 fl. oz / 1 cup of water and set it to the 'dough only' setting.

When the dough is ready, turn it out onto a lightly floured work surface and roll it into a fat sausage. Turn it 90⁰ and roll it tightly the other way, then transfer the dough to an oiled tin. Place the resrved tomatoes in a line along the top, pushing them into the dough.

Cover the tin loosely with oiled cling film and leave to prove somewhere warm for 1 hour.

Preheat the oven to 220⁰C (200⁰C fan) / 430F / gas 7.

Transfer the tin to the top shelf of the oven. Bake for 35–40 minutes or until the loaf sounds hollow when you tap it underneath. Transfer the bread to a wire rack and leave to cool completely before slicing.

Ingredients

200 g / 7 oz / 1 ⅓ cups strong white bread flour, plus extra for dusting

200 g / 7 oz / 1 ⅓ cups stoneground wholemeal flour

½ tsp easy-blend dried yeast

1 tbsp caster (superfine) sugar

1 tsp fine sea salt

150 g / 5 ½ oz / ¾ cup sun-dried tomatoes in oil, drained

1 tbsp olive oil

Bacon and Olive Bread

Makes: 1 loaf | Preparation time: 1 hour 30 minutes | Cooking time: 35 minutes

Ingredients

400 g / 14 oz / 2 ⅔ cups strong white bread flour, plus extra for dusting

½ tsp easy-blend dried yeast

1 tbsp caster (superfine) sugar

1 tsp fine sea salt

100 g / 3 ½ oz / 1 cup streaky bacon, chopped

75 g / 2 ½ oz / ½ cup black olives, pitted and chopped

Method

Measure all of the ingredients into the bread machine with 280 ml / 9 fl. oz / 1 cup of water and set it to the 'dough only' setting.

When the dough is ready, turn it out onto a lightly floured work surface and roll it into a fat sausage.

Turn it 90^0 and roll it tightly the other way then tuck the ends under and transfer the dough to a greased loaf tin, keeping the seam underneath. Cover the dough loosely with oiled cling film and leave to prove in a warm place for 45 minutes.

Preheat the oven to 220^{0}C (200^{0}c fan) / 430F / gas 7.

Transfer the tin to the top shelf of the oven. Bake for 35 minutes or until the underneath sounds hollow when tapped. Leave to cool completely on a wire rack before slicing.

Onion Bread

Makes: 1 loaf | Preparation time: 2 hours 15 minutes | Cooking time: 35–40 minutes

Method

Fry the onions in the oil for 15 minutes or until starting to caramelise. Leave to cool.

Measure the rest of the ingredients into the bread machine with 280 ml / 9 fl. oz / 1 cup of water and the fried onions and set it to the 'dough only' setting.

When the dough is ready, turn it out onto a lightly floured work surface and roll the dough into a fat sausage. Turn it 90⁰ and roll it tightly the other way then tuck the ends under and transfer the dough to a lined loaf tin, keeping the seam underneath. Cover the tin with oiled cling film and leave to prove for 1 hour.

Preheat the oven to 220⁰C (200⁰C fan) / 430 F / gas 7.

Bake the loaf for 35–40 minutes or until the underneath sounds hollow when tapped. Leave to cool completely on a wire rack before slicing.

Ingredients

2 large onions, peeled, quartered and sliced

3 tbsp olive oil

300 g / 10 ½ oz / 2 cups strong white bread flour, plus extra for dusting

100 g / 3 ½ oz / ⅔ cup stoneground wholemeal flour

½ tsp easy-blend dried yeast

1 tbsp caster (superfine) sugar

1 tsp fine sea salt

2 tbsp black onion seeds

Wholemeal Basil Bread

Makes: 1 loaf | Preparation time: 2 hours | Cooking time: 35–40 minutes

Ingredients

200 g / 7 oz / 1 ⅓ cups strong white bread flour, plus extra for dusting

200 g / 7 oz / 1 ⅓ cups stoneground wholemeal flour

½ tsp easy-blend dried yeast

1 tbsp caster (superfine) sugar

1 tsp fine sea salt

a small bunch of basil, chopped

3 tbsp olive oil

Method

Measure all of the ingredients into the bread machine with 280 ml / 9 fl. oz / 1 cup of water and set it to the 'dough only' setting.

When the dough is ready, turn it out onto a lightly floured work surface and roll it into a fat sausage. Turn it 90^0 and roll it tightly the other way, then tuck the ends under and transfer the dough to a square loaf tin. Cover the tin loosely with oiled cling film and leave to prove somewhere warm for 1 hour.

Preheat the oven to 220^0C (200^0C fan) / 430F / gas 7.

Transfer the tin to the top shelf of the oven. Bake for 35–40 minutes or until the loaf sounds hollow when you tap it underneath. Transfer the bread to a wire rack and leave to cool completely.

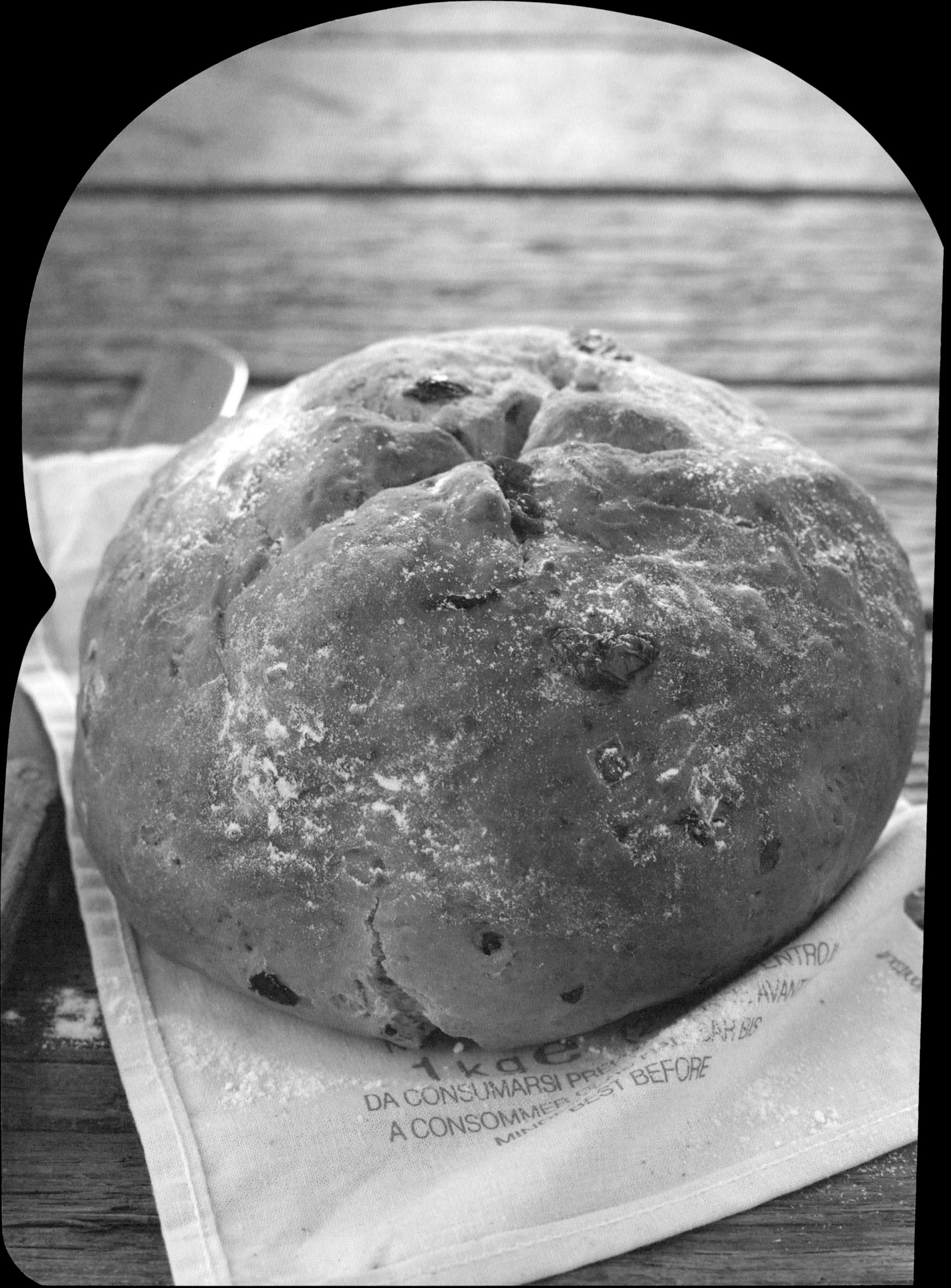
DA CONSUMARSI
BEST BEFORE
A CONSOMMER

Tomato and Olive Bread

Makes: 1 loaf | Preparation time: 2 hours | Cooking time: 35–40 minutes

Method

Measure all of the ingredients into the bread machine with 280 ml / 9 fl. oz / 1 cup of water and set it to the 'dough only' setting.

When the dough is ready, turn it out onto a lightly floured work surface. Cup your hands around the dough and move it in a circular motion whilst pressing down to form a tight round loaf.

Transfer the dough to a greased baking tray and cover with oiled cling film. Leave to prove for 1 hour or until doubled in size.

Meanwhile, preheat the oven to 220°C (200°C fan) / 425F / gas 7.

Slash a star in the top of the loaf with a sharp knife, then bake for 35–40 minutes or until the loaf sounds hollow when you tap it underneath. Transfer the bread to a wire rack and leave to cool completely before slicing.

Ingredients

400 g / 14 oz / 2 ⅔ cups strong white bread flour, plus extra for dusting

½ tsp easy-blend dried yeast

1 tbsp caster (superfine) sugar

1 tsp fine sea salt

100 g / 3 ½ oz / ⅔ cup black olives, pitted and chopped

100 g / 3 ½ oz / ½ cup sun-dried tomatoes in oil, drained

1 tbsp oil from the sun-dried tomato jar

Parmesan Loaf

Makes: 1 loaf | Preparation time: 2 hours | Cooking time: 35 minutes

Ingredients

400 g / 14 oz / 2 ⅔ cups strong white bread flour, plus extra for dusting

½ tsp easy-blend dried yeast

50 g / 1 ¾ oz / ½ cup parmesan, finely grated

1 tsp fine sea salt

1 tbsp olive oil

Method

Measure all of the ingredients into the bread machine with 280 ml / 9 fl. oz / 1 cup of water and set it to the 'dough only' setting.

When the dough is ready, turn it out onto a lightly floured work surface and press it out into a rectangle. Roll it up tightly and transfer to a lined loaf tin. Cover with oiled cling film and leave to prove for 1 hour or until doubled in size.

Preheat the oven to 220°C (200°C fan) / 425F / gas 7.

Bake for 35 minutes or until the loaf sounds hollow when you tap it underneath. Transfer to a wire rack and leave to cool completely before serving.

Saucisson Cobble Loaf

Makes: 1 | Preparation time: 2 hours | Cooking time: 40 minutes

Method

Measure all of the ingredients into the bread machine with 280 ml / 9 fl. oz / 1 cup of water and set it to the 'dough only' setting.

When the dough is ready, turn it out onto a lightly floured work surface. Shape the dough into a square loaf and transfer to a greased baking tray, then cover with oiled cling film and leave to prove for 1 hour or until doubled in size.

Preheat the oven to 220°C (200°C fan) / 425F / gas 7.

Transfer the tray to the top shelf of the oven.

Bake for 40 minutes or until the loaf sounds hollow when you tap it underneath. Transfer to a wire rack and leave to cool completely before serving.

Ingredients

400 g / 14 oz / 2 ⅔ cups strong white bread flour, plus extra for dusting

½ tsp easy-blend dried yeast

1 tsp fine sea salt

2 tbsp olive oil

100 g / 3 ½ oz / ½ cup saucisson, or salami, skinned and very thinly sliced

Olive Ciabatta Rolls

Makes: 3 | Preparation time: 2 hours | Cooking time: 15 minutes

Ingredients

100 g / 3 ½ oz / ⅔ cup strong white bread flour

200 g / 7 oz / 1 ⅓ cups of pasta flour, plus extra for dusting

½ tsp easy-blend dried yeast

1 tsp fine sea salt

2 tbsp olive oil

75 g / 2 ½ oz / ½ cup black olives, pitted and chopped

Method

Measure all of the ingredients into the bread machine with 200 ml / 7 fl. oz / ¾ cup of water and set it to the 'dough only' setting.

When the dough is ready, turn it out onto a lightly floured work surface. Press it out into a rectangle, then cut it into three rectangular rolls.

Transfer to an oiled baking tray, cover with oiled cling film and leave to prove for 1 hour or until doubled in size.

Meanwhile, preheat the oven to 220°C (200°C fan) / 425F / gas 7.

Bake for 15 minutes or until the underneaths sound hollow when you tap them. Transfer the rolls to a wire rack and leave to cool completely.

Cheese and Bacon Bread

Makes: 1 | Preparation time: 1 hour 30 minutes | Cooking time: 35 minutes

Method

Measure all of the ingredients into the bread machine with 280 ml / 9 fl. oz / 1 cup of water and set it to the 'dough only' setting.

When the dough is ready, turn it out onto a lightly floured work surface and roll it into a fat sausage.

Turn it 90⁰ and roll it tightly the other way then tuck the ends under and transfer the dough to a lined baking tray, keeping the seam underneath. Cover the dough loosely with oiled cling film and leave to prove in a warm place for 45 minutes.

Preheat the oven to 220⁰C (200⁰C fan) / 430F / gas 7.

Transfer the tray to the top shelf of the oven. Bake for 35 minutes or until the underneath sounds hollow when tapped. Leave to cool completely on a wire rack before slicing.

Ingredients

400 g / 14 oz / 2 ⅔ cups strong white bread flour, plus extra for dusting

½ tsp easy-blend dried yeast

1 tbsp caster (superfine) sugar

1 tsp fine sea salt

100 g / 3 ½ oz / 1 cup streaky bacon, chopped

100 g / 3 ½ oz / 1 cup Cheddar, grated

a small bunch of chives, chopped

Rye and Coriander Bread

Makes: 1 loaf | Preparation time: 3 hours | Cooking time: 35–40 minutes

Ingredients

400 g / 14 oz / 2 ⅔ cups rye flour, plus extra for dusting

1 tsp easy-blend dried yeast

1 tbsp treacle

1 tbsp malt extract

1 tsp fine sea salt

1 tbsp olive oil

2 tsp ground coriander (cilantro)

Method

Measure all of the ingredients into the bread machine with 280 ml / 9 fl. oz / 1 cup of water and set it to the 'dough only' setting.

When the dough is ready, turn it out onto a lightly floured work surface and shape it into a round loaf. Transfer the loaf to a greased baking tray and cover with oiled cling film. Leave to prove for 2 hours or until doubled in size.

Meanwhile, preheat the oven to 220ºC (200ºC fan) / 430F / gas 7 and dust the loaf with flour. Transfer the tray to the top shelf of the oven.

Bake for 35–40 minutes or until the loaf sounds hollow when tapped. Transfer the bread to a wire rack and leave to cool.

Parmesan Baguettes

Makes: 2 | Preparation time: 2 hours | Cooking time: 25 minutes

Method

Measure all of the ingredients into the bread machine with 280 ml / 9 fl. oz / 1 cup of water and set it to the 'dough only' setting.

When the dough is ready, turn it out onto a lightly floured work surface and roll it into two baguettes, tapering the ends to a point.

Transfer the baguettes to a greased baking tray then cover with oiled cling film and leave to prove for 1 hour or until doubled in size.

Preheat the oven to 220°C (200°C fan) / 425F / gas 7.

Dust the baguettes with a little flour and make a few diagonal slashes along the top with a sharp knife.

Bake for 25 minutes or until the baguettes sounds hollow when you tap them underneath. Transfer to a wire rack and leave to cool completely before serving.

Ingredients

350 g / 12 ½ oz / 1 ½ cups strong white bread flour, plus extra for dusting

50 g / 1 ¾ oz / ⅓ cup stoneground wholemeal flour

½ tsp easy-blend dried yeast

50 g / 1 ¾ oz / ½ cup parmesan, finely grated

1 tsp fine sea salt

1 tbsp olive oil

Onion and Poppy Seed Bread

Makes: 1 loaf | Preparation time: 2 hours 15 minutes | Cooking time: 35 minutes

Ingredients

400 g / 14 oz / 2 ⅔ cups strong white bread flour, plus extra for dusting

½ tsp easy-blend dried yeast

1 tbsp caster (superfine) sugar

1 tsp fine sea salt

1 tbsp olive oil

For the topping

1 onion, chopped

1 tbsp poppy seeds

Method

Measure all of the bread ingredients into the machine with 280 ml / 9 fl. oz / 1 cup of water and set it to the 'dough only' setting.

When the dough is ready, turn it out onto a lightly floured work surface. Sprinkle the onion over the bread, then knead it in until evenly mixed. Shape the bread into a round loaf and transfer to a greased baking tray. Cover the dough loosely with oiled cling film and leave to prove for 45 minutes.

Preheat the oven to 220⁰C (200⁰C fan) / 430F / gas 7.

Sprinkle the loaf with poppy seeds. Transfer the tray to the top shelf of the oven. Bake for 35 minutes or until the underneath sounds hollow when tapped. Leave to cool completely on a wire rack before slicing.

Bacon and Cheese Rolls

Makes: 8 rolls | Preparation time: 1 hour 45 minutes | Cooking time: 15–20 minutes

Method

Measure all of the ingredients except for the cheese into the bread machine with 280 ml / 9 fl. oz / 1 cup of water and set it to the 'dough only' setting.

When the dough is ready, turn it out onto a lightly floured work surface and divide it into eight rolls. Transfer the rolls to a greased baking tray, cover loosely with oiled cling film and leave to prove in a warm place for 45 minutes.

Preheat the oven to 220⁰C (200⁰C fan) / 430F / gas 7.

Top half of the rolls with grated Gouda and the rest with the Fourme d'Ambert slices. Bake for 15 –20 minutes or until the underneaths sounds hollow when tapped. Leave to cool for at least 10 minutes before serving.

Ingredients

400 g / 14 oz / 2 ⅔ cups strong white bread flour, plus extra for dusting

½ tsp easy-blend dried yeast

1 tbsp caster (superfine) sugar

1 tsp fine sea salt

100 g / 3 ½ oz / 1 cup streaky bacon, chopped

50 g / 1 ¾ oz / ½ cup Gouda, grated

4 slices Fourme d'Ambert

Cheese and Chive Cob

Makes: 1 | Preparation time: 2 hours 30 minutes | Cooking time: 55 minutes

Ingredients

400 g / 14 oz / 2 ⅔ cups strong white bread flour, plus extra for dusting

½ tsp easy-blend dried yeast

1 tbsp caster (superfine) sugar

1 tsp fine sea salt

1 tbsp olive oil

For the filling

150 g / 5 ½ oz / 1 ½ cups Cheddar, sliced

a small bunch of chives, chopped

Method

Measure all of the ingredients into the bread machine with 280 ml / 9 fl. oz / 1 cup of water and set it to the 'dough only' setting.

When the dough is ready, shape it into a round cob loaf and transfer to a greased baking tray. Cover with oiled cling film and leave to prove for 1 hour or until doubled in size.

Preheat the oven to 220°C (200°C fan) / 425F / gas 7.

Bake for 40 minutes or until the loaf sounds hollow when you tap it underneath. Transfer to a wire rack and leave to cool for 20 minutes.

Cut a cross-hatch pattern into the bread without cutting all the way through and stuff with the cheese and chives. Return the bread to the oven for 15 minutes or until the cheese has melted. Serve warm.

Sweet
Bread

Raisin Batons

Makes: 2 | Preparation time: 2 hours | Cooking time: 30 minutes

Ingredients

200 g / 7 oz / 1 ⅓ cups strong white bread flour

200 g / 7 oz / 1 ⅓ cups stoneground wholemeal flour

½ tsp easy-blend dried yeast

2 tbsp caster (superfine) sugar

1 tsp fine sea salt

1 tbsp olive oil

75 g / 2 ½ oz / ⅓ cup raisins

Method

Measure all of the ingredients into the bread machine with 280 ml / 9 fl. oz / 1 cup of water and set it to the 'dough only' setting.

When the dough is ready, turn it out onto a lightly floured work surface then divide it into two pieces and shape into fat batons. Transfer the batons to a greased baking tray and cover with oiled cling film. Leave to prove for 1 hour or until doubled in size.

Meanwhile, preheat the oven to 220°C (200°C fan) / 425F / gas 7.

Make two diagonal slashes across the top of each baton with a sharp knife. Transfer the tray to the top shelf of the oven.

Bake for 30 minutes or until the loaves sound hollow when you tap them underneath. Transfer to a wire rack and leave to cool completely.

Prune and Sultana Loaf

Makes: 1 loaf | Preparation time: 2 hours | Cooking time: 35–40 minutes

Ingredients

400 g / 14 oz / 2 ⅔ cups strong white bread flour, plus extra for dusting

½ tsp easy-blend dried yeast

1 tbsp caster (superfine) sugar

1 tsp fine sea salt

100 g / 3 ½ oz / ½ cup sultanas

1 tbsp butter, melted

For the prune ripple

150 g / 5 ½ oz / ¾ cup stoned prunes

1 tsp ground cinnamon

4 tbsp apple juice

Method

Measure all of the ingredients for the dough mixture into the bread machine with 280 ml / 9 fl. oz / 1 cup of water and set it to the 'dough only' setting.

Put the prunes, cinnamon and apple juice in a food processor and blend to a smooth paste.

When the dough is ready, turn it out onto a lightly floured work surface. Knead through the prune paste to ripple, then press it into a rectangle, roll it up and transfer to a greased loaf tin. Cover with oiled cling film and leave to prove for 1 hour or until doubled in size.

Meanwhile, preheat the oven to 220°C (200°C fan) / 425F / gas 7.

Transfer the tin to the top shelf of the oven. Bake for 35–40 minutes or until the loaf sounds hollow when tapped.

Raisin and Apple Bread

Makes: 1 loaf | Preparation time: 2 hours | Cooking time: 35–40 minutes

Ingredients

1 eating apple

400 g / 14 oz / 2 ⅔ cups strong white bread flour, plus extra for dusting

½ tsp easy-blend dried yeast

2 tbsp caster (superfine) sugar

1 tsp ground cinnamon

1 tsp fine sea salt

100 g / 3 ½ oz / ½ cup raisins

1 tbsp butter, melted

Method

Cut a slice from the middle of the apple and reserve, then peel and coarsely grate the rest.

Measure all of the ingredients into the bread machine with 280 ml / 9 fl. oz / 1 cup of water and the grated apple, and set it to the 'dough only' setting.

When the dough is ready, turn it out onto an oiled baking tray and shape it into a round loaf. Cover with oiled cling film and leave to prove for 1 hour or until doubled in size.

Meanwhile, preheat the oven to 220°C (200°C fan) / 425F / gas 7.

When the dough has risen, slash a cross in the top and lay the apple slice on top. Transfer the tray to the top shelf of the oven.

Bake for 35–40 minutes or until the loaf sounds hollow when tapped.

Fig and Muesli Bread

Makes: 1 | Preparation time: 2 hours | Cooking time: 40 minutes

Method

Measure all of the ingredients into the bread machine with 280 ml / 9 fl. oz / 1 cup of water and set it to the 'dough only' setting.

When the dough is ready, turn it out onto a lightly floured work surface and shape into a long loaf. Transfer the loaf to a greased baking tray and cover with oiled cling film. Leave to prove for 1 hour or until doubled in size.

Preheat the oven to 220⁰C (200⁰C fan) / 430F / gas 7.

Slash a diamond pattern into the top with a sharp knife. Transfer the tray to the top shelf of the oven.

Bake for 35–40 minutes or until the loaf sounds hollow when you tap it underneath. Transfer to a wire rack and leave to cool.

Ingredients

350 g / 12 ½ oz / 2 ⅓ cups strong white bread flour, plus extra for dusting

50 g / 1 ¾ oz / ⅓ cup stoneground wholemeal flour

75 g / 2 ½ oz / ¾ cup muesli

½ tsp easy-blend dried yeast

1 tbsp caster (superfine) sugar

1 tsp fine sea salt

1 tbsp olive oil

3 fresh figs, chopped

Sweet Poppy Seed Loaf

Makes: 1 loaf | Preparation time: 2 hours | Cooking time: 35–40 minutes

Ingredients

400 g / 14 oz / 2 ⅔ cups strong white bread flour, plus extra for dusting

1 tsp easy-blend dried yeast

4 tbsp caster (superfine) sugar

1 tsp fine sea salt

3 tbsp butter, melted

280 ml / 9 fl. oz / 1 ¼ cups whole milk

1 tbsp poppy seeds

Method

Measure all of the ingredients except for the poppy seeds into the bread machine and set it to the 'dough only' setting.

When the dough is ready, turn it out onto a lightly floured work surface. Press it into a rectangle, then roll it up and transfer to a greased loaf tin. Cover with oiled cling film and leave to prove for 1 hour or until doubled in size.

Meanwhile, preheat the oven to 220°C (200°C fan) / 425F / gas 7.

Sprinkle the top with poppy seeds. Transfer the tin to the top shelf of the oven. Bake for 35–40 minutes or until the loaf sounds hollow when tapped.

Cranberry and Almond Loaf

Makes: 1 | Preparation time: 2 hours | Cooking time: 35–40 minutes

Method

Measure all of the ingredients into the bread machine and set it to the 'dough only' setting.

When the dough is ready, turn it out onto a lightly floured work surface. Press it into a rectangle, then roll it up and transfer to a greased loaf tin. Cover with oiled cling film and leave to prove for 1 hour or until doubled in size.

Meanwhile, preheat the oven to 220°C (200°C fan) / 425F / gas 7.

Transfer the tin to the top shelf of the oven. Bake for 35–40 minutes or until the loaf sounds hollow when tapped.

Ingredients

400 g / 14 oz / 2 ⅔ cups strong white bread flour, plus extra for dusting

1 tsp easy-blend dried yeast

4 tbsp caster (superfine) sugar

1 tsp fine sea salt

100 g / 3 ½ oz / ½ cup dried cranberries

75 g / 2 ½ oz / 1 cup flaked (slivered) almonds

3 tbsp butter, melted

280 ml / 10 fl. oz / 1 ¼ cups whole milk

Small Plum Cobs

Makes: 2 | Preparation time: 2 hours | Cooking time: 25–30 minutes

Ingredients

400 g / 14 oz / 2 ⅔ cups strong white bread flour, plus extra for dusting

½ tsp easy-blend dried yeast

1 tbsp caster (superfine) sugar

1 tsp fine sea salt

1 tbsp olive oil

3 plums, quartered and stoned

Method

Measure all of the ingredients except for the plums into the bread machine with 280 ml / 9 fl. oz / 1 cup of water and set it to the 'dough only' setting.

When the dough is ready, turn it out onto a lightly floured work surface and knead in the plums. Split the dough in half and shape into two round loaves.

Transfer the cobs to a greased baking tray and cover with oiled cling film. Leave to prove for 1 hour or until doubled in size.

Meanwhile, preheat the oven to 220°C (200°C fan) / 425F / gas 7.

Dust the cobs with flour and slash a pattern in the tops with a knife.

Bake for 25–30 minutes or until the loaves sound hollow when you tap them underneath. Transfer to a wire rack and leave to cool.

Apple Bread

Makes: 1 loaf | Preparation time: 2 hours | Cooking time: 35–40 minutes

Method

Measure all of the ingredients into the bread machine with 280 ml / 9 fl. oz / 1 cup of water and set it to the 'dough only' setting.

When the dough is ready, turn it out onto an oiled baking tray and shape it into a long loaf. Cover with oiled cling film and leave to prove for 1 hour or until doubled in size.

Meanwhile, preheat the oven to 220°C (200°C fan) / 425F / gas 7.

When the dough has risen, slash the top with a sharp knife. Transfer the tray to the top shelf of the oven.

Bake for 35–40 minutes or until the loaf sounds hollow when tapped.

Ingredients

400 g / 14 oz / 2 ⅔ cups strong white bread flour, plus extra for dusting

½ tsp easy-blend dried yeast

2 tbsp caster (superfine) sugar

1 tsp ground ginger

1 tsp fine sea salt

1 eating apple, peeled, cored and chopped

1 tbsp butter, melted

Raisin and Cinnamon Bread

Makes: 1 loaf | Preparation time: 2 hours | Cooking time: 35–40 minutes

Ingredients

400 g / 14 oz / 2 ⅔ cups strong
white bread flour, plus
extra for dusting

½ tsp easy-blend dried yeast

1 tbsp caster (superfine) sugar

1 tsp ground cinnamon

1 tsp fine sea salt

100 g / 3 ½ oz / ½ cup raisins

1 tbsp butter, melted

1 egg, beaten

Method

Measure all of the ingredients except for the egg into the bread machine with 280 ml / 9 fl. oz / 1 cup of water and set it to the 'dough only' setting.

When the dough is ready, turn it out onto a lightly floured work surface. Press it into a rectangle, then roll it up and transfer to a greased loaf tin. Cover with oiled cling film and leave to prove for 1 hour or until doubled in size.

Meanwhile, preheat the oven to 220°C (200°C fan) / 425F / gas 7.

When the dough has risen, brush the top with beaten egg and score a diamond pattern across the top. Transfer the tin to the top shelf of the oven. Bake for 35–40 minutes or until the loaf sounds hollow when tapped.

Nutty
Loaves

Fig and Walnut Bread

Makes: 1 loaf | Preparation time: 2 hours | Cooking time: 35–40 minutes

Method

Measure all of the ingredients into the bread machine with 280 ml / 9 fl. oz / 1 cup of water and set it to the 'dough only' setting.

When the dough is ready, turn it out onto a lightly floured work surface. Cup your hands around the dough and move it in a circular motion whilst pressing down to form a tight round loaf.

Transfer the dough to a greased baking tray and cover with oiled cling film. Leave to prove for 1 hour or until doubled in size then slash a cross in the top.

Preheat the oven to 220⁰C (200⁰C fan) / 430F / gas 7.

Bake for 35–40 minutes or until the loaf sounds hollow when tapped. Transfer the bread to a wire rack and leave to cool completely before slicing.

Ingredients

400 g / 14 oz / 2 ⅔ cups strong white bread flour, plus extra for dusting

½ tsp easy-blend dried yeast

1 tbsp caster (superfine) sugar

1 tsp fine sea salt

100 g / 3 ½ oz / ½ cup dried figs, chopped

100 g / 3 ½ oz / ¾ cup walnut halves

Cinnamon and Walnut Bread

Makes: 1 loaf | Preparation time: 2 hours 15 minutes | Cooking time: 35–40 minutes

Ingredients

100 g / 3 ½ oz / ¾ cup walnut halves

200 g / 7 oz / 1 ⅓ cups strong white bread flour

200 g / 7 oz / 1 ⅓ cups rye flour, plus extra for dusting

½ tsp easy-blend dried yeast

1 tbsp caster (superfine) sugar

1 tsp ground cinnamon

1 tsp fine sea salt

1 tbsp walnut oil

Method

Reserve a third of the walnuts, then measure everything into the bread machine with 280 ml / 9 fl. oz / 1 cup of water and set it to the 'dough only' setting.

When the dough is ready, turn it out onto a lightly floured work surface. Shape the loaf and transfer to a loaf tin. Cover with oiled cling film and leave to prove for 1 hour or until doubled in size.

Preheat the oven to 220⁰C (200⁰C fan) / 430F / gas 7.

When the dough has risen, dust the top with rye flour and stud with the reserved walnut halves.

Transfer the tin to the top shelf of the oven.

Bake for 35–40 minutes or until the loaf sounds hollow when tapped. Transfer the bread to a wire rack and leave to cool.

Chestnut, Rye and Wheat Bread

Makes: 1 loaf | Preparation time: 2 hours | Cooking time: 35–40 minutes

Method

Measure all of the ingredients into the bread machine with 280 ml / 9 fl. oz / 1 cup of water and set it to the 'dough only' setting, using the 'wholemeal' option if available.

When the dough is ready, turn it out onto a lightly floured work surface and shape it into a round loaf. Transfer the loaf to a greased baking tray and cover with oiled cling film. Leave to prove for 1 hour or until doubled in size.

Meanwhile, preheat the oven to 220⁰C (200⁰C fan) / 430F / gas 7.

When the dough has risen, score the top with a knife and dust with flour. Transfer the tray to the top shelf of the oven.

Bake for 35–40 minutes or until the loaf sounds hollow when tapped. Transfer the bread to a wire rack and leave to cool.

Ingredients

200 g / 7 oz / 1 ⅓ cups strong white bread flour, plus extra for dusting

100 g / 3 ½ oz / ⅔ cup rye flour

100 g / 3 ½ oz / ⅔ cup chestnut flour

1 tsp easy-blend dried yeast

1 tbsp caster (superfine) sugar

1 tsp fine sea salt

1 tbsp olive oil

Honey, Walnut and Almond Loaf

Makes: 1 loaf | Preparation time: 2 hours | Cooking time: 35–40 minutes

Ingredients

200 g / 7 oz / 1 ⅓ cups strong white bread flour

200 g / 7 oz / 1 ⅓ cups stoneground wholemeal flour

3 tbsp ground almonds

1 tsp easy-blend dried yeast

3 tbsp runny honey

1 tsp fine sea salt

1 tbsp olive oil

For the topping

2 tbsp runny honey

25 g / 1 oz / ½ cup blanched almonds, roughly chopped

25 g / 1 oz / ½ cup walnuts, roughly chopped

Method

Measure all of the bread ingredients into the machine with 280 ml / 9 fl. oz / 1 cup of water and set it to the 'dough only' setting.

When the dough is ready, turn it out onto a lightly floured work surface and roll it into a fat sausage. Turn it 90⁰ and roll it tightly the other way, then tuck the ends under and transfer the dough to an oiled loaf tin. Cover the tin loosely with oiled cling film and leave to prove somewhere warm for 1 hour.

Preheat the oven to 220⁰C (200⁰C fan) / 430F / gas 7.

Bake for 35–40 minutes or until the loaf sounds hollow when you tap it underneath. Transfer the bread to a wire rack, then brush with honey and sprinkle over the nuts. Leave to cool completely before slicing.

Fig and Hazelnut Bread

Makes: 1 loaf | Preparation time: 2 hours | Cooking time: 35–40 minutes

Method

Measure all of the ingredients into the bread machine with 280 ml / 9 fl. oz / 1 cup of water and set it to the 'dough only' setting.

When the dough is ready, turn it out onto a lightly floured work surface and shape into a long loaf. Transfer the loaf to a greased baking tray and cover with oiled cling film. Leave to prove for 1 hour or until doubled in size.

Preheat the oven to 220°C (200°C fan) / 430F / gas 7.

Make a long slash down the centre with a sharp knife. Transfer the tray to the top shelf of the oven.

Bake for 35–40 minutes or until the loaf sounds hollow when you tap it underneath. Transfer to a wire rack and leave to cool.

Ingredients

350 g / 12 ½ oz / 2 ⅓ cups strong white bread flour, plus extra for dusting

50 g / 1 ¾ oz / ⅓ cup stoneground wholemeal flour

3 fresh figs, chopped

75 g / 2 ½ oz / ⅔ cup hazelnuts (cob nuts), roughly chopped

½ tsp easy-blend dried yeast

1 tbsp caster (superfine) sugar

1 tsp fine sea salt

1 tbsp olive oil

Walnut and Raisin Bread

Makes: 1 loaf | Preparation time: 2 hours | Cooking time: 35 minutes

Ingredients

400 g / 14 oz / 2 ⅔ cups strong white bread flour, plus extra for dusting

1 tsp easy-blend dried yeast

4 tbsp light brown sugar

1 tsp fine sea salt

100 g / 3 ½ oz / ¾ cup walnuts, chopped

100 g / 3 ½ oz / ½ cup raisins

2 tbsp butter, melted

2 tbsp sugar nibs

Method

Measure all of the ingredients, except for the sugar nibs, into the bread machine with 280 ml / 9 fl. oz / 1 cup of water and set it to the 'dough only' setting.

When the dough is ready, turn it out onto a lightly floured work surface and shape it into a long loaf. Transfer the loaf to a greased baking tray and cover again with oiled cling film. Leave to prove for 1 hour or until doubled in size.

Meanwhile, preheat the oven to 220°C (200°C fan) / 425F / gas 7.

When the dough has risen, sprinkle the top with sugar nibs. Transfer the tray to the top shelf of the oven.

Bake for 35 minutes or until the loaf sounds hollow when tapped, then leave to cool completely on a wire rack.

Raisin, Walnut and Rye Batons

Makes: 2 | Preparation time: 2 hours | Cooking time: 30 minutes

Method

Measure all of the ingredients into the bread machine with 280 ml / 9 fl. oz / 1 cup of water and set it to the 'dough only' setting.

When the dough is ready, turn it out onto a lightly floured work surface then divide it into two pieces and shape into fat batons. Transfer the batons to a greased baking tray and cover with oiled cling film. Leave to prove for 1 hour or until doubled in size.

Meanwhile, preheat the oven to 220°C (200°C fan) / 425F / gas 7.

Make diagonal slashes down both sides of each baton with a sharp knife. Transfer the tray to the top shelf of the oven.

Bake for 30 minutes or until the loaves sound hollow when you tap them underneath. Transfer to a wire rack and leave to cool completely.

Ingredients

200 g / 7 oz / 1 ⅓ cups strong white bread flour, plus extra for dusting

200 g / 7 oz / 1 ⅓ cups rye flour

1 tsp easy-blend dried yeast

3 tbsp runny honey

1 tsp fine sea salt

1 tbsp butter, melted

1 tsp mixed spice

75 g / 2 ½ oz / ½ cup raisins

75 g / 2 ½ oz / ⅔ cup walnuts, chopped

Crusty Walnut Rolls

Makes: 12 | Preparation time: 2 hours | Cooking time: 12 minutes

Ingredients

200 g / 7 oz / 1 ⅓ cups strong white bread flour, plus extra for dusting

200 g / 7 oz / 1 ⅓ cups stoneground wholemeal flour

½ tsp easy-blend dried yeast

1 tbsp caster (superfine) sugar

75 g / 2 ½ oz / ⅔ cup walnuts, chopped

1 tsp fine sea salt

2 tbsp walnut oil

Method

Measure all of the ingredients into the bread machine with 280 ml / 9 fl. oz / 1 cup of water and set it to the 'dough only' setting.

When the dough is ready, turn it out onto a lightly floured work surface. Roll out the dough into a square, then cut it into 12 rectangular rolls and transfer to a greased baking tray. Cover the rolls with oiled cling film and leave to prove for 1 hour or until doubled in size.

Preheat the oven to 220°C (200°C fan) / 430F / gas 7.

Transfer the tray to the top shelf of the oven. Bake for 12 minutes or until the rolls sound hollow when you tap them underneath.

Shaped
Breads

Granary Mini Loaves

Makes: 6 | Preparation time: 1 hour 45 minutes | Cooking time: 20 minutes

Ingredients

400 g / 14 oz / 2 ⅔ cups granary bread flour

½ tsp easy-blend dried yeast

1 tbsp caster (superfine) sugar

1 tsp fine sea salt

1 tbsp olive oil

Method

Measure all of the ingredients into the bread machine with 280 ml / 9 fl. oz / 1 cup of water and set it to the 'dough only' setting.

When the dough is ready, turn it out onto a lightly floured work surface. Divide the dough into six equal pieces and transfer to six lined mini bamboo loaf trays. Transfer the loaves to a baking tray, cover with oiled cling film and leave to prove for 45 minutes or until doubled in size.

Preheat the oven to 220°C (200°C fan) / 425F / gas 7.

Transfer the baking tray to the top shelf of the oven. Bake for 20 minutes or until the loaves sounds hollow when you tap them underneath. Transfer to a wire rack and leave to cool completely before serving.

Leaf Breads

Makes: 2 | Preparation time: 2 hours | Cooking time: 30 minutes

Method

Measure all of the ingredients into the bread machine with 280 ml / 9 fl. oz / 1 cup of water and set it to the 'dough only' setting.

When the dough is ready, turn it out onto a lightly floured work surface then divide it into two pieces and shape into fat batons. Transfer the batons to a greased baking tray and cover with oiled cling film. Leave to prove for 1 hour or until doubled in size.

Meanwhile, preheat the oven to 220°C (200°C fan) / 425F / gas 7.

Slash a leaf vein pattern into the top of each baton with a sharp knife. Transfer the tray to the top shelf of the oven.

Bake for 30 minutes or until the loaves sound hollow when you tap them underneath. Transfer to a wire rack and leave to cool completely.

Ingredients

400 g / 14 oz / 2 ⅔ cups strong white bread flour

½ tsp easy-blend dried yeast

2 tbsp caster (superfine) sugar

1 tsp fine sea salt

1 tbsp olive oil

Farmhouse Baguette

Makes: 1 | Preparation time: 2 hours | Cooking time: 20–30 minutes

Ingredients

150 g / 5 ½ oz / 1 cup strong white bread flour, plus extra for dusting

50 g / 1 ¾ oz / ⅓ cup stoneground wholemeal flour

½ tsp easy-blend dried yeast

1 tbsp caster (superfine) sugar

1 tsp fine sea salt

1 tbsp olive oil

Method

Measure all of the ingredients into the bread machine with 140 ml of water and set it to the 'dough only' setting.

When the dough is ready, turn it out onto a lightly floured work surface and roll the dough into a long baguette. Transfer it to a greased baking tray, cover with oiled cling film and leave to prove for 1 hour or until doubled in size.

Preheat the oven to 220°C (200°C fan) / 430F / gas 7.

Dust the baguette with flour and make diagonal slashes along the top with a sharp knife. Transfer the tray to the top shelf of the oven.

Bake for 20–30 minutes or until the baguette sounds hollow when you tap it underneath. Transfer to a wire rack and leave to cool.

White Floured Rolls

Makes: 12 | Preparation time: 2 hours 30 minutes | Cooking time: 12 minutes

Method

Measure all of the ingredients into the bread machine with 280 ml / 9 fl. oz / 1 cup of water and set it to the 'dough only' setting.

When the dough is ready, turn it out onto a lightly floured work surface. Divide the dough into twelve pieces and shape into balls, then transfer to a greased baking tray. Cover the rolls with oiled cling film and leave to prove for 1 hour or until doubled in size.

Preheat the oven to 220°C (200°C fan) / 430F / gas 7.

Cut a circle in the top of each roll with a sharp knife. Transfer the tray to the top shelf of the oven. Bake for 12 minutes or until the rolls sound hollow when you tap them underneath.

Ingredients

400 g / 14 oz / 2 ⅔ cups strong white bread flour, plus extra for dusting

½ tsp easy-blend dried yeast

1 tbsp caster (superfine) sugar

1 tsp fine sea salt

1 tbsp olive oil

Soft Sesame Pretzels

Makes: 8 | Preparation time: 2 hours 30 minutes | Cooking time: 10–15 minutes

Ingredients

450 g / 1lb / 3 cups strong white bread flour

1 tsp easy-blend dried yeast

1 tbsp caster (superfine) sugar

1 tsp fine sea salt

4 tbsp bicarbonate of (baking) soda

1 egg, beaten

3 tbsp sesame seeds

Method

Measure all of the ingredients except the egg, sesame seeds and bicarbonate of soda, into the bread machine with 280 ml / 9 fl. oz / 1 cup of water and set it to the 'dough only' setting.

When the dough is ready, divide it into eight pieces and roll each one into a long rope. Curl the dough into your desired shape and squeeze the ends to seal.

Cover the pretzels with oiled cling film and leave to prove for 1 hour or until doubled in size.

Meanwhile, preheat the oven to 220°C (200°C fan) / 425F / gas 7.

Bring 1 litre of water to the boil and stir in the bicarbonate of soda. Blanch the pretzels in batches for 1 minute then transfer to two oiled baking trays.

Brush the pretzels with beaten egg and sprinkle with sesame seeds then bake for 10–15 minutes or until cooked through and golden brown. Leave to cool for a few minutes before serving.

Fougasse

Makes: 1 | Preparation time: 2 hours | Cooking time: 25 minutes

---

Method

Measure all of the ingredients into the bread machine with 280 ml / 9 fl. oz / 1 cup of water and set it to the 'dough only' setting.

When the dough is ready, turn it out onto a lightly floured work surface and shape it into a leaf, making deep slashes where the veins would be. Transfer the fougasse to a greased baking tray then cover with oiled cling film and leave to prove for 1 hour or until doubled in size.

Preheat the oven to 220°C (200°C fan) / 425F / gas 7.

Transfer the tray to the top shelf of the oven.

Bake for 25 minutes or until the bread sounds hollow when you tap it underneath. Transfer to a wire rack and leave to cool completely before serving.

Ingredients

200 g / 7 oz / 1 ⅓ cups strong white bread flour, plus extra for dusting

½ tsp easy-blend dried yeast

1 tsp fine sea salt

3 tbsp olive oil

Tomato and Olive Snake Loaf

Makes: 2 loaves | Preparation time: 2 hours | Cooking time: 35 minutes

Ingredients

400 g / 14 oz / 2 ⅔ cups strong white bread flour, plus extra for dusting

½ tsp easy-blend dried yeast

1 tbsp caster (superfine) sugar

1 tsp fine sea salt

100 g / 3 ½ oz / ⅔ cup mixed olives, pitted and sliced

100 g / 3 ½ oz / ½ cup sun-dried tomatoes in oil, drained and finely chopped

1 tbsp oil from the sun-dried tomatoes

Method

Measure all of the ingredients into the bread machine with 280 ml / 9 fl. oz / 1 cup of water and set it to the 'dough only' setting.

When the dough is ready, turn it out onto a lightly floured work surface, then shape it into two fat sausages. Fold each sausage round into an 'S' shape then transfer to a greased baking tray and cover with oiled cling film. Leave to prove for 1 hour or until doubled in size.

Meanwhile, preheat the oven to 220°C (200°C fan) / 425F / gas 7.

Transfer the tray to the top shelf of the oven.

Bake for 35 minutes or until the loaves sound hollow when you tap them underneath. Transfer to a wire rack and leave to cool completely.

Satellite Bread

Makes: 1 loaf | Preparation time: 2 hours | Cooking time: 25–35 minutes

Method

Measure all of the ingredients into the bread machine with 280 ml / 9 fl. oz / 1 cup of water and set it to the 'dough only' setting.

When the dough is ready, pull off three pieces of dough for the satellite rolls and shape the rest into a round loaf. Transfer to a greased baking tray and arrange the rolls round the outside, then cover with oiled cling film and leave to prove for 1 hour or until doubled in size.

Preheat the oven to 220°C (200°C fan) / 430F / gas 7.

Dust with flour and slash the top with a knife. Transfer the tray to the top shelf of the oven.

Bake for 25–30 minutes or until the loaf sounds hollow when tapped underneath. Transfer to a wire rack and leave to cool.

Ingredients

400 g / 14 oz / 2 ⅔ cups strong white bread flour, plus extra for dusting

½ tsp easy-blend dried yeast

1 tbsp caster (superfine) sugar

1 tsp fine sea salt

1 tbsp olive oil

Spelt Batons

Makes: 2 | Preparation time: 2 hours | Cooking time: 30 minutes

Ingredients

400 g / 14 oz / 2 ⅔ cups white spelt flour

½ tsp easy-blend dried yeast

2 tbsp caster (superfine) sugar

1 tsp fine sea salt

1 tbsp olive oil

Method

Measure all of the ingredients into the bread machine with 280 ml / 9 fl. oz / 1 cup of water and set it to the 'dough only' setting.

When the dough is ready, turn it out onto a lightly floured work surface then divide it into two pieces and shape into fat batons. Transfer the batons to a greased baking tray and cover with oiled cling film. Leave to prove for 1 hour or until doubled in size.

Meanwhile, preheat the oven to 220°C (200°C fan) / 425F / gas 7.

Make two slashes across the top of each baton with a sharp knife. Transfer the tray to the top shelf of the oven.

Bake for 30 minutes or until the loaves sound hollow when you tap them underneath. Transfer to a wire rack and leave to cool completely.

Flat
Breads

Cumin Seed Naan

Makes: 4 | Preparation time: 1 hour 15 minutes | Cooking time: 8 minutes

Ingredients

2 tsp cumin seeds

250 g / 9 oz / 1 ⅔ cups strong white bread flour, plus extra for dusting

½ tsp easy-blend dried yeast

1 tsp caster (superfine) sugar

½ tsp fine sea salt

1 tbsp vegetable oil

2 tbsp natural yoghurt

melted butter for brushing

Method

Dry fry the cumin seeds for 2 minutes or until fragrant, then grind to a rough powder.

Measure all of the ingredients except for the butter into the bread machine with 100 ml / 3 ½ fl.oz / ½ cup of water and the cumin and set it to the 'dough only' setting.

When the dough is ready, turn it out onto a lightly floured work surface, divide it into four pieces and roll each one out into a rough circle.

Heat a large ovenproof heavy-based frying pan on the hob for a few minutes and preheat the grill.

Lay the first naan in the frying pan, then transfer the pan to the grill. Cook for 1–2 minutes or until the surface is puffy and golden brown and the bread is cooked through underneath.

Repeat with the rest of the naan, starting the pan off on the hob as before. Brush the breads with melted butter and serve as soon as possible.

Naan Bread

Makes: 4 | Preparation time: 1 hour 15 minutes | Cooking time: 8 minutes

Method

Measure all of the ingredients except for the butter into the bread machine with 100 ml / 3 ½ fl.oz / ½ cup of water and the cumin seeds and set it to the 'dough only' setting.

When the dough is ready, turn it out onto a lightly floured work surface, divide it into four pieces and roll each one out into a rough oval.

Heat a large ovenproof heavy-based frying pan on the hob for a few minutes and preheat the grill.

Lay the first naan in the frying pan, then transfer the pan to the grill and cook for 1–2 minutes or until the surface is puffy and golden brown and the bread is cooked through underneath.

Repeat with the rest of the naan, starting the pan off on the hob as before. Brush the breads with melted butter and serve as soon as possible.

Ingredients

250 g / 9 oz / 1 ⅔ cups strong white bread flour, plus extra for dusting

½ tsp easy-blend dried yeast

1 tsp caster (superfine) sugar

½ tsp fine sea salt

1 tbsp vegetable oil

2 tbsp natural yoghurt

melted butter for brushing

1 tbsp cumin seeds

Olive and Rosemary Focaccia

Makes: 3 | Preparation time: 2 hours | Cooking time: 25 minutes

Ingredients

150 g / 5 ½ oz / 1 cup strong white bread flour

150 g / 5 ½ oz / 1 cup stoneground wholemeal flour

½ tsp easy-blend dried yeast

1 tsp fine sea salt

2 tbsp olive oil, plus extra for drizzling

75 g / 2 ½ oz / ½ cup black olives, pitted and chopped

2 tbsp rosemary, chopped

Method

Measure all of the ingredients into the bread machine with 280 ml / 9 fl.oz of water and set it to the 'dough only' setting.

When the dough is ready, turn it out onto a lightly floured work surface. Oil a baking tray then divide the dough into three and roll into long ovals. Cover the focaccia with oiled cling film and leave to prove for 1 hour or until doubled in size.

Preheat the oven to 220°C (200°C fan) / 430F / gas 7. Make dimples over the surface of the dough with your finger.

Transfer the tray to the top shelf of the oven and close the door. Bake for 25 minutes or until the top is golden and the base is cooked through. Drizzle with oil then leave to cool completely on a wire rack.

Pine Nut Focaccia

Makes: 1 | Preparation time: 2 hours | Cooking time: 25 minutes

Method

Measure all of the ingredients except for the pine nuts, into the bread machine with 280 ml / 9 fl.oz of water and set it to the 'dough only' setting.

When the dough is ready, turn it out onto a lightly floured work surface. Line a baking tray then stretch out the dough into a long oval. Cover the focaccia with oiled cling film and leave to prove for 1 hour or until doubled in size.

Preheat the oven to 220°C (200°C fan) / 430F / gas 7. Scatter the pine nuts over the top of the focaccia.

Transfer the tray to the top shelf of the oven and close the door. Bake for 25 minutes or until the top is golden and the base is cooked through. Leave to cool completely on a wire rack.

Ingredients

250 g / 9 oz / 1 ⅔ cups strong white bread flour

50 g / 1 ¾ oz / ⅓ cup stoneground wholemeal flour

½ tsp easy-blend dried yeast

1 tsp fine sea salt

2 tbsp olive oil

75 g / 2 ½ oz / ⅔ cup pine nuts

Cherry Tomato and Rosemary Focaccia

Makes: 1 | Preparation time: 2 hours | Cooking time: 25 minutes

Ingredients

250 g / 9 oz / 1 ⅔ cups strong white bread flour

50 g / 1 ¾ oz / ⅓ cup stoneground wholemeal flour

½ tsp easy-blend dried yeast

1 tsp fine sea salt

2 tbsp olive oil

75 g / 2 ½ oz / ⅓ cup sun-dried tomatoes in oil, drained and chopped

1 tbsp rosemary, roughly chopped

9 cherry tomatoes

sea salt crystals for sprinkling

Method

Measure all of the ingredients except for the cherry tomatoes into the bread machine with 280 ml / 9 fl.oz of water and set it to the 'dough only' setting.

When the dough is ready, turn it out onto a lightly floured work surface. Oil a baking tray then stretch out the dough into a circle and stud with the tomatoes. Cover the focaccia with oiled cling film and leave to prove for 1 hour or until doubled in size.

Preheat the oven to 220°C (200°C fan) / 430 F / gas 7.

Transfer the tray to the top shelf of the oven and close the door. Bake for 25 minutes or until the top is golden and the base is cooked through. Leave to cool completely on a wire rack then serve sprinkled with sea salt crystals.

Onion Focaccia

Makes: 1 | Preparation time: 2 hours | Cooking time: 25 minutes

Method

Measure all of the ingredients into the bread machine with 280 ml / 9 fl.oz of water and set it to the 'dough only' setting.

Oil a rectangular cake tin then stretch out the dough to cover the base. Cover with oiled cling film and leave to prove for 1 hour or until doubled in size.

Preheat the oven to 220°C (200°C fan) / 430F / gas 7.

Sprinkle the onion and thyme over the top of the focaccia. Put the oil, water and salt in a jam jar and shake well to emulsify. Pour it all over the dough.

Transfer the tin to the top shelf of the oven and close the door.

Bake for 25 minutes or until the top is golden and the base is cooked through. Leave to cool on a wire rack before cutting into squares.

Ingredients

300 g / 10 ½ oz / 2 cups strong white bread flour

½ tsp easy-blend dried yeast

1 tsp fine sea salt

2 tbsp olive oil

To finish:

1 onion, quartered and thinly sliced

1 tbsp thyme leaves

50 ml / 1 ¾ fl. oz / ¼ cup olive oil

50 ml / 1 ¾ fl. oz / ¼ cup warm water

½ tsp fine sea salt

Grape and Rosemary Focaccia

Makes: 1 | Preparation time: 2 hours 15 minutes | Cooking time: 25 minutes

Ingredients

300 g / 10 ½ oz / 2 cups strong white bread flour

½ tsp easy-blend dried yeast

1 tsp fine sea salt

2 tbsp olive oil

To finish:

75 g / 2 ½ oz / ½ cup seedless red grapes

1 tbsp rosemary

50 ml / 1 ¾ fl. oz / ¼ cup olive oil

50 ml / 1 ¾ fl. oz / ¼ cup warm water

½ tsp sea salt crystals

Method

Measure all of the ingredients except for the cherry tomatoes into the bread machine with 280 ml / 9 fl.oz of water and set it to the 'dough only' setting.

When the dough is ready, turn it out onto a lightly floured work surface. Oil a rectangular cake tin then stretch out the dough to cover the base. Cover the focaccia with oiled cling film and leave to prove for 1 hour or until doubled in size.

Preheat the oven to 220°C (200°C fan) / 430 F / gas 7.

Sprinkle the grapes and rosemary over the top of the focaccia and press down lightly. Put the oil, water and salt in a jam jar and shake well to emulsify. Pour it all over the dough.

Bake for 25 minutes or until the top is golden and the base is cooked through. Leave to cool on a wire rack before cutting into squares.

Tomato and Anchovy Focaccia

Makes: 1 | Preparation time: 1 hour 30 minutes | Cooking time: 15 minutes

Method

Measure all of the ingredients into the machine with 140 ml / 4 ½ fl.oz of water and set it to the 'dough only' setting.

Preheat the oven to 220°C (200°C fan) / 430F / gas 7 and grease a non-stick baking tray.

When the dough is ready, turn it out onto a lightly floured work surface and press or roll it out into a circle.

Transfer the circle to the baking tray and spread with pizza sauce. Arrange the anchovies, olives and garlic on top, then leave to rise for 15 minutes.

Transfer the tray to the oven and bake for 15 minutes or until the focaccia is cooked through underneath.

Ingredients

200 g / 7 oz / 1 ⅓ cups strong white bread flour, plus extra for dusting

½ tsp easy-blend dried yeast

1 tsp caster (superfine) sugar

½ tsp fine sea salt

1 tbsp olive oil, plus extra for drizzling

For the topping:

3 tbsp tomato pizza sauce

10 salted anchovy fillets, rinsed

5 black olives

1 clove of garlic, sliced

Roquefort and Butternut filled Focaccia

Makes: 1 | Preparation time: 2 hours | Cooking time: 25 minutes

Ingredients

200 g / 7 oz / 1 ⅓ cups strong white bread flour, plus extra for dusting

½ tsp easy-blend dried yeast

1 tsp caster (superfine) sugar

½ tsp fine sea salt

1 tbsp olive oil, plus extra for drizzling

For the filling:

150 g / 5 ½ oz / ⅔ cup Roquefort, sliced

200 g / 7 oz / 1 ½ cups steamed butternut squash, cooled

a handful of sage leaves, chopped

Method

Measure all of the ingredients into the bread machine with 140 ml / 4 ½ fl.oz of water and set it to the 'dough only' setting.

Preheat the oven to 220°C (200°C fan) / 430F / gas 7.

When the dough is ready, turn it out onto a lightly floured work surface and press or roll it out into a rectangle.

Transfer the rectangle to the baking tray and top one half with the butternut squash, Roquefort and sage. Fold over the bread and crimp the edges to seal, then leave to rise for 45 minutes.

Lay a doily on top of the dough and dust over a little flour. Transfer the tray to the oven and bake for 25 minutes or until the focaccia is cooked through underneath. Serve warm.

Rosemary Focaccia

Makes: 1 | Preparation time: 2 hours 15 minutes | Cooking time: 25 minutes

Method

Measure all of the dough ingredients into the bread machine with 280 ml / 9 fl.oz of water and set it to the 'dough only' setting.

Oil a rectangular cake tin then scrape in the dough and stretch out to cover the base. Cover the focaccia with oiled cling film and leave to prove for 1 hour or until doubled in size.

Preheat the oven to 220°C (200°C fan) / 430F / gas 7.

Put the oil, water and salt in a jam jar and shake well to emulsify. Pour it all over the dough then sprinkle with the rosemary.

Bake for 25 minutes or until the top is golden and the base is cooked through. Leave to cool on a wire rack before cutting into squares.

Ingredients

300 g / 10 ½ oz / 2 cups strong white bread flour

½ tsp easy-blend dried yeast

1 tsp fine sea salt

2 tbsp olive oil

To finish:

50 ml / 1 ¾ fl. oz / ¼ cup olive oil

50 ml / 1 ¾ fl. oz / ¼ cup warm water

½ tsp fine sea salt

1 tsp dried rosemary

Fennel Seed Focaccia

Makes: 1 | Preparation time: 2 hours | Cooking time: 25 minutes

Ingredients

250 g / 9 oz / 1 ⅔ cups strong white bread flour

50 g / 1 ¾ oz / ⅓ cup stoneground wholemeal flour

½ tsp easy-blend dried yeast

2 tsp fennel seeds, ground to a fine powder

1 tsp fine sea salt

2 tbsp olive oil

Method

Measure all of the ingredients into the bread machine with 280 ml / 9 fl.oz of water and set it to the 'dough only' setting.

When the dough is ready, turn it out onto a lightly floured work surface. Oil a baking tray then stretch out the dough into a rectangle. Cover the focaccia with oiled cling film and leave to prove for 1 hour or until doubled in size.

Preheat the oven to 220°C (200°C fan) / 430F / gas 7.

Transfer the tray to the top shelf of the oven and close the door. Bake for 25 minutes or until the top is golden and the base is cooked through. Leave to cool completely on a wire rack.

Rustic Focaccia

Makes: 1 | Preparation time: 2 hours | Cooking time: 25 minutes

Method

Measure all of the ingredients into the bread machine with 280 ml / 9 fl.oz of water and set it to the 'dough only' setting.

When the dough is ready, turn it out onto a lightly floured work surface. Oil a baking tray then stretch out the dough into a circle. Cover the focaccia with oiled cling film and leave to prove for 1 hour or until doubled in size.

Preheat the oven to 220°C (200°C fan) / 430F / gas 7. Make dimples over the surface of the bread with your finger.

Transfer the tray to the top shelf of the oven and close the door. Bake for 25 minutes or until the top is golden and the base is cooked through. Leave to cool completely on a wire rack.

Ingredients

250 g / 9 oz / 1 ⅔ cups strong white bread flour

50 g / 1 ¾ oz / ⅓ cup stoneground wholemeal flour

½ tsp easy-blend dried yeast

1 tsp fine sea salt

2 tbsp olive oil

Prosciutto and Gorgonzola filled Focaccia

Makes: 1 | Preparation time: 2 hours | Cooking time: 25 minutes

Ingredients

200 g / 7 oz / 1 ⅓ cups strong white bread flour, plus extra for dusting

½ tsp easy-blend dried yeast

1 tsp caster (superfine) sugar

½ tsp fine sea salt

1 tbsp olive oil, plus extra for drizzling

For the filling:

150 g / 5 ½ oz / ⅔ cup gorgonzola, sliced

6 slices prosciutto, chopped

a handful of basil leaves, chopped

Method

Measure all of the bread ingredients into the bread machine with 140 ml / 4 ½ fl.oz of water and set it to the 'dough only' setting.

Preheat the oven to 220°C (200°C fan) / 430F / gas 7.

When the dough is ready, turn it out onto a lightly floured work surface and press or roll it out into a rectangle.

Transfer the rectangle to the baking tray and top one half with the gorgonzola, prosciutto and basil. Fold over the bread and crimp the edges to seal, then leave to rise for 45 minutes.

Transfer the tray to the oven and bake for 25 minutes or until the focaccia is cooked through underneath.

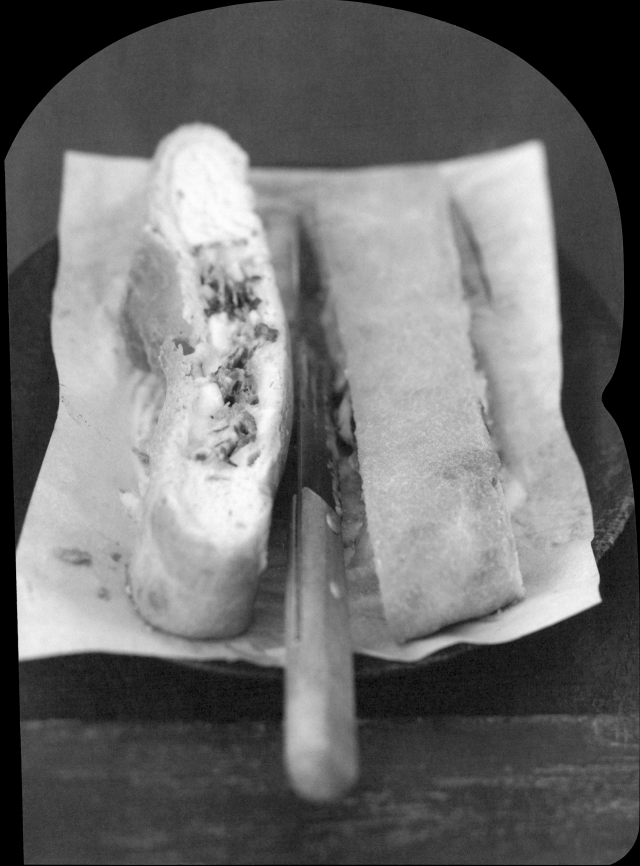

Unusual
Breads

Garlic Mushroom Bread

Makes: 1 loaf | Preparation time: 2 hours 30 minutes | Cooking time: 35–40 minutes

Ingredients

200 g / 7 oz / 1 ⅓ cups strong white bread flour

200 g / 7 oz / 1 ⅓ cups rye flour

1 tsp easy-blend dried yeast

1 tbsp caster (superfine) sugar

1 tsp fine sea salt

1 tbsp olive oil

For the mushrooms:

50 g / 1 ¾ oz / ¼ cup butter

300 g / 10 ½ oz / 4 cups chestnut mushrooms, sliced

2 cloves of garlic, crushed

25 g / 1 oz / 1 cup flat leaf parsley, chopped

Method

Measure all of the bread ingredients into the bread machine with 280 ml / 9 fl.oz of water and set it to the 'dough only' setting.

Meanwhile, melt the butter in a sauté pan then add the mushrooms and plenty of salt and pepper. Fry for 10 minutes, then add the garlic and parsley and cook for 2 minutes. Leave to cool.

When the dough is ready, turn it out onto a lightly floured work surface and knead the mushrooms into the dough. Shape into a square loaf then transfer to a greased baking tray, cover with oiled cling film and prove until doubled in size.

Preheat the oven to 220°C (200°C fan) / 430F / gas 7.

Transfer the tray to the top shelf of the oven and bake for 35–40 minutes or until the loaf sounds hollow when tapped. Transfer the bread to a wire rack and leave to cool.

Curry and Pistachio Bread

Makes: 1 loaf | Preparation time: 2 hours | Cooking time: 35–40 minutes

Method

Measure all of the ingredients into the bread machine with 280 ml / 9 fl.oz / 1 cup of water and set it to the 'dough only' setting.

When the dough is ready, turn it out onto a lightly floured work surface and roll it into a fat sausage. Turn it 90° and roll it tightly the other way then tuck the ends under and transfer the dough to the tin, keeping the seam underneath.

Cover the tin with oiled cling film and leave to prove for 1 hour.

Preheat the oven to 220°C (200°C fan) / 430F / gas 7.

Transfer the tin to the top shelf of the oven and close the door.

Bake for 35–40 minutes or until the underneath sounds hollow when tapped. Leave to cool completely on a wire rack.

Ingredients

300 g / 10 ½ oz / 2 cups strong white bread flour, plus extra for dusting

100 g / 3 ½ oz / ⅔ cup stoneground wholemeal flour

½ tsp easy-blend dried yeast

1 tbsp caster (superfine) sugar

1 tsp fine sea salt

2 tbsp mild curry powder

75 g / 2 ½ oz / ⅔ cup pistachio nuts, roughly chopped

2 tbsp olive oil

Yoghurt Bread

Makes: 2 loaves | Preparation time: 2 hours | Cooking time: 30 minutes

Ingredients

300 g / 10 ½ oz / 2 cups strong white bread flour, plus extra for dusting

½ tsp easy-blend dried yeast

1 tbsp caster (superfine) sugar

1 tsp fine sea salt

300 ml / 10 ½ fl. oz / 1 ¼ cups natural yoghurt, plus extra for brushing

Method

Measure all of the ingredients into the bread machine and set it to the 'dough only' setting.

When the dough is ready, turn it out onto a lightly floured work surface, divide the dough in half and shape each piece into a square loaf. Transfer to a greased baking tray, cover with oiled cling film and leave to prove for 1 hour or until doubled in size.

Meanwhile, preheat the oven to 220°C (200°C fan) / 430F / gas 7.

Brush the top of the loaves with yoghurt or leave them plain. Bake for 30 minutes or until the loaves sound hollow when you tap them underneath. Transfer to a wire rack and leave to cool completely.

Beer Bread

Makes: 1 | Preparation time: 2 hours | Cooking time: 40 minutes

Method

Measure all of the ingredients into the bread machine and set it to the 'dough only' setting.

When the dough is ready, turn it out onto a lightly floured work surface. Shape the dough into an oval loaf and transfer to a greased baking tray, then cover with oiled cling film and leave to prove for 1 hour or until doubled in size.

Preheat the oven to 220°C (200°C fan) / 430F / gas 7.

Transfer the tray to the top shelf of the oven and close the door.

Bake for 40 minutes or until the loaf sounds hollow when you tap it underneath. Transfer to a wire rack and leave to cool completely before serving.

Ingredients

400 g / 14 oz / 2 ⅔ cups strong white bread flour, plus extra for dusting

½ tsp easy-blend dried yeast

1 tbsp caster (superfine) sugar

1 tsp fine sea salt

1 tbsp olive oil

280 ml / 10 fl. oz / 1 ¼ cup beer

White chocolate Ciabatta Rolls

Makes: 4 | Preparation time: 2 hours | Cooking time: 15 minutes

Ingredients

100 g / 3 ½ oz / ⅔ cup strong white bread flour

200 g / 7 oz / 1 ⅓ cups of pasta flour, plus extra for dusting

½ tsp easy-blend dried yeast

2 tbsp caster (superfine) sugar

1 tsp fine sea salt

2 tbsp olive oil

75 g / 2 ½ oz / ½ cup white chocolate buttons

Method

Measure all of the ingredients into the bread machine with 200 ml / 7 fl.oz of water and set it to the 'dough only' setting.

When the dough is ready, turn it out onto a lightly floured work surface. Press it out into a rectangle, then cut it into quarters.

Transfer to an oiled baking tray, cover with oiled cling film and leave to prove for 1 hour or until doubled in size.

Meanwhile, preheat the oven to 220°C (200° fan) / 425F / gas 7.

Bake for 15 minutes or until the underneaths sound hollow when you tap them. Transfer the rolls to a wire rack and leave to cool completely.

Mixed Herb Ciabatta Rolls

Makes: 4 | Preparation time: 2 hours | Cooking time: 15 minutes

Method

Pound the herbs with a pestle and mortar until pulped, then stir in the oil.

Measure all of the ingredients into the bread machine with 200 ml / 7 fl.oz of water and the herb oil set it to the 'dough only' setting.

When the dough is ready, turn it out onto a lightly floured work surface. Press it out into a rectangle, then cut it into quarters.

Transfer the rolls to an oiled baking tray, cover with oiled cling film and leave to prove for 1 hour or until doubled in size.

Meanwhile, preheat the oven to 220°C (200°C fan) / 430F / gas 7.

Bake for 15 minutes or until the underneaths sound hollow when you tap them. Transfer the rolls to a wire rack and leave to cool completely.

Ingredients

1 tbsp oregano leaves

1 tbsp flat leaf parsley, chopped

½ tbsp thyme leaves

½ tbsp sage leaves, chopped

1 tsp rosemary leaves, chopped

2 tbsp olive oil

100 g / 3 ½ oz / ⅔ cup strong white bread flour

200 g / 7 oz / 1 ⅓ cups of pasta flour, plus extra for dusting

½ tsp easy-blend dried yeast

1 tsp fine sea salt

Chocolate and Dried Strawberry Bread

Makes: 2 loaves | Preparation time: 2 hours | Cooking time: 35 minutes

Ingredients

400 g / 14 oz / 2 ⅔ cups strong white bread flour, plus extra for dusting

1 tsp easy-blend dried yeast

4 tbsp light brown sugar

1 tsp fine sea salt

50 g / 1 ¾ oz / ½ cup unsweetened cocoa powder

100 g / 3 ½ oz / ½ cup dried strawberries

2 tbsp butter, melted

Method

Measure all of the ingredients into the bread machine with 280 ml / 9 fl.oz of water and set it to the 'dough only' setting.

When the dough is ready, turn it out onto a lightly floured work surface and shape it into two loaves. Transfer the loaves to a greased baking tray and cover with oiled cling film. Leave to prove for 1 hour or until doubled in size.

Meanwhile, preheat the oven to 220°C (200°C fan) / 430F / gas 7.

Transfer the tray to the top shelf of the oven and close the door. Bake for 35 minutes or until the loaves sound hollow when tapped. Leave to cool completely on a wire rack.

Milk Rolls

Makes: 9 | Preparation time: 2 hours 30 minutes | Cooking time: 12 minutes

Method

Measure all of the ingredients except for the egg and sugar nibs into the bread machine and set it to the 'dough only' setting.

When the dough is ready, turn it out onto a lightly floured work surface. Divide the dough into nine pieces and shape into balls, then transfer to a greased baking tray. Cover the rolls with oiled cling film and leave to prove for 1 hour or until doubled in size.

Preheat the oven to 220°C (200°C fan) / 430F / gas 7.

Snip a pattern into the top of each roll with scissors, then brush with egg and sprinkle with sugar nibs. Transfer the tray to the top shelf of the oven.

Bake for 12 minutes or until the rolls sound hollow when you tap them underneath.

Ingredients

400 g / 14 oz / 2 ⅔ cups strong white bread flour, plus extra for dusting

½ tsp easy-blend dried yeast

1 tbsp caster (superfine) sugar

1 tsp fine sea salt

1 tbsp olive oil

280 ml / 10 fl. oz / 1 ¼ cups milk

1 egg, beaten

3 tbsp sugar nibs

Green Tea Bread

Makes: 1 | Preparation time: 2 hours | Cooking time: 40 minutes

Ingredients

400 g / 14 oz / 2 ⅔ cups strong white bread flour, plus extra for dusting

½ tsp easy-blend dried yeast

1 tbsp caster (superfine) sugar

2 tbsp matcha green tea powder

1 tsp fine sea salt

1 tbsp olive oil

Method

Measure all of the ingredients into the bread machine with 280 ml / 9 fl.oz of water and set it to the 'dough only' setting.

When the dough is ready, turn it out onto a lightly floured work surface. Roll the dough into a fat sausage and transfer it to a greased loaf tin. Cover with oiled cling film and leave to prove for 1 hour or until doubled in size.

Preheat the oven to 220°C (200°C fan) / 425F / gas 7.

Transfer the tin to the top shelf of the oven and close the door.

Bake for 40 minutes or until the loaf sounds hollow when you tap it underneath. Transfer to a wire rack and leave to cool completely before serving.

Rye and Sunflower Bread

Makes: 1 | Preparation time: 3 hours | Cooking time: 30–35 minutes

Method

Measure all of the ingredients into the bread machine with 300 ml / 10 fl.oz of water and set it to the 'dough only' setting.

When the dough is ready, scrape it into a shallow rectangular baking tray and cover with oiled cling film. Leave to prove for 2 hours or until doubled in size.

Meanwhile, preheat the oven to 220°C (200°C fan) / 430 F / gas 7.

Transfer the tray to the top shelf of the oven then close the door.

Bake for 30–35 minutes or until the loaf sounds hollow when tapped. Transfer the bread to a wire rack and leave to cool.

Ingredients

400 g / 14 oz / 2 ⅔ cups dark rye flour

1 tsp easy-blend dried yeast

1 tbsp treacle

1 tbsp malt extract

1 tsp fine sea salt

1 tbsp sunflower oil

50 g / 1 ¾ oz / ½ cup sunflower seeds

1 tsp ground coriander (cilantro)

Rye and Poppy Seed Morteau Bread

Makes: 1 loaf | Preparation time: 2 hours 15 minutes | Cooking time: 35–40 minutes

Ingredients

200 g / 7 oz / 1 ⅓ cups rye flour

200 g / 7 oz / 1 ⅓ cups stoneground wholemeal flour

1 tsp easy-blend dried yeast

1 tbsp caster (superfine) sugar

3 tbsp poppy seeds

1 tsp fine sea salt

1 tbsp olive oil

1 large or 2 small morteau sausages

Method

Measure all of the ingredients except for the sausage into the bread machine with 280 ml / 9 fl.oz of water and set it to the 'dough only' setting.

Press the dough out into a rough rectangle, then lay the sausage on top and fold over the dough. Transfer to an oiled baking tray, cover with oiled cling film and leave to prove for 1 hour or until doubled in size.

Preheat the oven to 220°C (200°C fan) / 430 F / gas 7.

Transfer the tin to the top shelf of the oven then close the door.

Bake for 35–40 minutes or until the loaf sounds hollow when tapped. Transfer the bread to a wire rack and leave to cool.

Rice Bread

Makes: 1 loaf | Preparation time: 2 hours | Cooking time: 35–40 minutes

Method

Measure all of the ingredients into the bread machine with 280 ml / 9 fl.oz of water and set it to the 'dough only' setting.

When the dough is ready, turn it out onto a lightly floured work surface and roll the dough into a fat sausage. Turn it 90° and roll it tightly the other way then tuck the ends under and transfer the dough to a greased loaf tin, keeping the seam underneath. Cover the tin with cling film and leave to prove for 1 hour or until doubled in size.

Meanwhile, preheat the oven to 220°C (200°C fan) / 430F / gas 7.

Bake for 35–40 minutes or until the loaf sounds hollow when you tap it underneath. Transfer the bread to a wire rack and leave to cool completely before slicing.

Ingredients

300 g / 10 ½ oz / 2 cups strong white bread flour, plus extra for dusting

½ tsp easy-blend dried yeast

1 tbsp caster (superfine) sugar

1 tsp fine sea salt

300 g / 10 ½ oz / 1 ¾ cups cooked white rice, cooled

1 tbsp olive oil

Sandwich
Breads

Wholemeal Oat Rolls

Makes: 9 rolls | Preparation time: 2 hours | Cooking time: 12 minutes

Method

Measure all of the bread ingredients into the machine with 280 ml / 9 fl. oz / 1 cup of water and set it to the 'dough only' setting, using the 'wholemeal' option if available.

When the dough is ready, turn it out onto a lightly floured work surface. Divide the dough into nine pieces and shape into balls, then transfer to a greased baking tray. Cover the rolls with oiled cling film and leave to prove for 1 hour or until doubled in size.

Preheat the oven to 220°C (200°C fan) / 430F / gas 7.

Brush the rolls with milk, then sprinkle with oats to coat. Transfer the tray to the top shelf of the oven.

Bake for 12 minutes or until the rolls sound hollow when you tap them underneath.

Ingredients

200 g / 7 oz / 1 ⅓ cups strong white bread flour, plus extra for dusting

200 g / 7 oz / 1 ⅓ cups stoneground wholemeal flour

½ tsp easy-blend dried yeast

1 tbsp caster (superfine) sugar

1 tsp fine sea salt

2 tbsp olive oil

For the topping

2 tbsp milk

4 tbsp porridge oats

Floured Cob

Makes: 1 | Preparation time: 2 hours | Cooking time: 40 minutes

Ingredients

400 g / 14 oz / 2 ⅔ cups strong white bread flour, plus extra for dusting

½ tsp easy-blend dried yeast

1 tbsp caster (superfine) sugar

1 tsp fine sea salt

1 tbsp olive oil

Method

Measure all of the ingredients into the bread machine with 280 ml / 9 fl.oz of water and set it to the 'dough only' setting.

When the dough is ready, turn it out onto a lightly floured work surface. Shape the dough into a round cob loaf and transfer to a greased baking tray, then cover with oiled cling film and leave to prove for 1 hour or until doubled in size.

Preheat the oven to 220°C (200°C fan) / 425F / gas 7.

Dust the loaf with flour. Transfer the tray to the top shelf of the oven then close the door. Bake for 40 minutes or until the loaf sounds hollow when you tap it underneath. Transfer to a wire rack and leave to cool completely before serving.

Wholemeal Cob Rolls

Makes: 9 rolls | Preparation time: 2 hours | Cooking time: 12 minutes

Method

Measure all of the ingredients into the bread machine with 280 ml / 9 fl.oz of water and set it to the 'dough only' setting, using the 'wholemeal' option if available.

When the dough is ready, turn it out onto a lightly floured work surface. Divide the dough into nine pieces and shape into balls, then transfer to a greased baking tray. Cover the rolls with oiled cling film and leave to prove for 1 hour or until doubled in size.

Preheat the oven to 220°C (200°C fan) / 430F / gas 7.

Cut a cross in the top of each roll with a sharp knife. Transfer the tray to the top shelf of the oven then close the door. Bake for 12 minutes or until the rolls sound hollow when you tap them underneath.

Ingredients

200 g / 7 oz / 1 ⅓ cups strong white bread flour, plus extra for dusting

200 g / 7 oz / 1 ⅓ cups stoneground wholemeal flour

½ tsp easy-blend dried yeast

1 tbsp caster (superfine) sugar

1 tsp fine sea salt

2 tbsp olive oil

2 tbsp milk

Half and Half Batons

Makes: 2 | Preparation time: 2 hours | Cooking time: 30 minutes

Ingredients

200 g / 7 oz / 1 ⅓ cups strong white bread flour

200 g / 7 oz / 1 ⅓ cups stoneground wholemeal flour

½ tsp easy-blend dried yeast

2 tbsp caster (superfine) sugar

1 tsp fine sea salt

1 tbsp olive oil

Method

Measure all of the ingredients into the bread machine with 280 ml / 9 fl.oz of water and set it to the 'dough only' setting.

When the dough is ready, turn it out onto a lightly floured work surface then divide it into two pieces and shape into fat batons. Transfer the batons to a greased baking tray and cover with oiled cling film. Leave to prove for 1 hour or until doubled in size.

Meanwhile, preheat the oven to 220°C (200°C fan) / 430F / gas 7.

Make two diagonal slashes across the top of each baton with a sharp knife. Transfer the tray to the top shelf of the oven.

Bake for 30 minutes or until the loaves sound hollow when you tap them underneath. Transfer to a wire rack and leave to cool completely.

Wholemeal Granary Batons

Makes: 2 | Preparation time: 2 hours | Cooking time: 30 minutes

Method

Measure all of the ingredients into the bread machine with 280 ml / 9 fl. oz of water and set it to the 'dough only' setting.

When the dough is ready, turn it out onto a lightly floured work surface then divide it into two pieces and shape into fat batons. Transfer the batons to a greased baking tray and cover with oiled cling film. Leave to prove for 1 hour or until doubled in size.

Meanwhile, preheat the oven to 220°C (200°C fan) / 430F / gas 7.

Make two diagonal slashes across the top of each baton with a sharp knife. Transfer the tray to the top shelf of the oven and close the door.

Bake for 30 minutes or until the loaves sound hollow when you tap them underneath. Transfer to a wire rack and leave to cool completely.

Ingredients

200 g / 7 oz / 1 ⅓ cups malted granary flour

200 g / 7 oz / 1 ⅓ cups wholemeal bread flour

½ tsp easy-blend dried yeast

2 tbsp caster (superfine) sugar

1 tsp fine sea salt

1 tbsp olive oil

Sesame Granary Bread

Makes: 1 | Preparation time: 2 hours | Cooking time: 30 minutes

Ingredients

200 g / 7 oz / 1 ⅓ cups malted granary flour

200 g / 7 oz / 1 ⅓ cups string white bread flour

½ tsp easy-blend dried yeast

2 tbsp caster (superfine) sugar

1 tsp fine sea salt

1 tbsp sesame oil

1 tbsp milk

2 tbsp sesame seeds

Method

Measure all of the ingredients, except for the milk and sesame seeds, into the bread machine with 280 ml / 9 fl.oz of water and set it to the 'dough only' setting.

When the dough is ready, turn it out onto a lightly floured work surface and shape it into a long loaf. Cover with oiled cling film and leave to prove for 1 hour or until doubled in size.

Meanwhile, preheat the oven to 220°C (200°C fan) / 430F / gas 7.

Brush the loaf with milk and sprinkle with sesame seeds. Transfer the tray to the top shelf of the oven and close the door.

Bake for 30 minutes or until the loaf sounds hollow when you tap it underneath. Transfer to a wire rack and leave to cool completely.

Wholemeal Poppy Seed Loaf

Makes: 1 | Preparation time: 2 hours | Cooking time: 35–40 minutes

Method

Measure all of the ingredients into the bread machine with 280 ml / 9 fl. oz / 1 cup of water and set it to the 'dough only' setting.

When the dough is ready, turn it out onto a lightly floured work surface and shape it into a round loaf on a greased baking tray.

Cover with oiled cling film and leave to prove for 1 hour or until doubled in size.

Meanwhile, preheat the oven to 220⁰C (200⁰C fan) / 430F / gas 7.

Sprinkle the loaf with poppy seeds. Transfer the tray to the top shelf of the oven.

Bake for 35–40 minutes or until the loaf sounds hollow when you tap it underneath. Transfer to a wire rack and leave to cool.

Ingredients

300 g / 10 ½ oz / 2 cups stoneground wholemeal flour

100 g / 3 ½ oz / ⅔ cup strong white bread flour, plus extra for dusting

½ tsp easy-blend dried yeast

2 tbsp caster (superfine) sugar

1 tsp fine sea salt

1 tbsp olive oil

3 tbsp poppy seeds

Linseed Batons

Makes: 4 | Preparation time: 2 hours 30 minutes | Cooking time: 20 minutes

Method

Measure all of the ingredients into the bread machine with 280 ml / 9 fl.oz of water and set it to the 'dough only' setting.

When the dough is ready, turn it out onto a lightly floured work surface then then divide it into four pieces and shape into batons. Transfer the batons to a greased baking tray and cover with oiled cling film. Leave to prove for 1 hour or until doubled in size.

Meanwhile, preheat the oven to 220°C (200°C fan) / 430F / gas 7.

Make two diagonal slashes across the top of each baton with a sharp knife. Transfer the tray to the top shelf of the oven and close the door.

Bake for 20 minutes or until the loaves sound hollow when you tap them underneath. Transfer to a wire rack and leave to cool completely.

Ingredients

400 g / 14 oz / 2 ⅔ cups strong white bread flour, plus extra for dusting

½ tsp easy-blend dried yeast

2 tbsp caster (superfine) sugar

1 tsp fine sea salt

25 g / 1 oz / ¼ cup linseeds

1 tbsp linseed oil

Small Poppy Seed Cobs

Makes: 3 | Preparation time: 2 hours | Cooking time: 20–30 minutes

Ingredients

300 g / 10 ½ oz / 2 cups strong white bread flour

1 tsp easy-blend dried yeast

1 tbsp caster (superfine) sugar

1 tsp fine sea salt

1 tbsp olive oil

2 tbsp milk

3 tbsp poppy seeds

Method

Measure all of the ingredients, except for the milk and poppy seeds, into the bread machine with 210 ml / 7 fl.oz of water and set it to the 'dough only' setting.

When the dough is ready, turn it out onto a lightly floured work surface and divide it into three. Shape each piece into a cob, then transfer them to a greased baking tray, cover with oiled cling film and leave to prove for 1 hour or until doubled in size.

Preheat the oven to 220°C (200°C fan) / 430 F / gas 7.

Brush the cobs with milk and sprinkle with poppy seeds. Transfer the tray to the top shelf of the oven close the door.

Bake for 20–30 minutes or until the cobs sound hollow when you tap them underneath. Transfer to a wire rack and leave to cool.

Crusty Torpedo Rolls

Makes: 6 | Preparation time: 2 hours | Cooking time: 20 minutes

Method

Measure all of the ingredients into the bread machine with 280 ml / 9 fl.oz of water and set it to the 'dough only' setting.

When the dough is ready, turn it out onto a lightly floured work surface. Shape the dough into 6 torpedo-shaped rolls and transfer to a greased baking tray, then cover with oiled cling film and leave to prove for 1 hour or until doubled in size.

Preheat the oven to 220°C (200°C fan) / 430F / gas 7.

Dust the rolls with flour and slash the top of each one diagonally with a sharp knife. Transfer the tray to the top shelf of the oven and close the door.

Bake for 20 minutes or until the rolls sound hollow when you tap them underneath. Transfer to a wire rack and leave to cool completely before serving.

Ingredients

400 g / 14 oz / 2 ⅔ cups strong white bread flour, plus extra for dusting

½ tsp easy-blend dried yeast

1 tbsp caster (superfine) sugar

1 tsp fine sea salt

1 tbsp olive oil

Poppy Seed Baguette

Makes: 1 | Preparation time: 2 hours | Cooking time: 20–30 minutes

Ingredients

200 g / 7 oz / 1 ⅓ cups strong white bread flour

½ tsp easy-blend dried yeast

1 tbsp caster (superfine) sugar

1 tsp fine sea salt

1 tbsp olive oil

3 tbsp poppy seeds

Method

Measure all of the ingredients except for the poppy seeds into the bread machine with 140 ml / 4 ½ fl.oz of water and set it to the 'dough only' setting.

When the dough is ready, turn it out onto a lightly floured work surface and roll into a long baguette. Roll the baguette in the poppy seeds, then transfer to a greased baking tray, cover with oiled cling film and leave to prove for 1 hour or until doubled in size.

Preheat the oven to 220°C (200°C fan) / 430F / gas 7.

Make diagonal slashes along the top of the baguette with a sharp knife. Transfer the tray to the top shelf of the oven and close the door.

Bake for 20–30 minutes or until the baguette sounds hollow when you tap it underneath. Transfer to a wire rack and leave to cool.

Floured Wholemeal Cob

Makes: 1 | Preparation time: 2 hours | Cooking time: 40 minutes

Method

Measure all of the ingredients into the bread machine with 280 ml / 9 fl.oz of water and set it to the 'dough only' setting.

When the dough is ready, turn it out onto a lightly floured work surface. Shape the dough into a round cob loaf and transfer to a greased baking tray, then cover with oiled cling film and leave to prove for 1 hour or until doubled in size.

Preheat the oven to 220°C (200°C fan) / 430F / gas 7.

Dust the loaf with flour. Transfer the tray to the top shelf of the oven then close the door. Bake for 40 minutes or until the loaf sounds hollow when you tap it underneath. Transfer to a wire rack and leave to cool completely before serving.

Ingredients

200 g / 7 oz / 1 ⅓ cups strong white bread flour, plus extra for dusting

200 g / 7 oz / 1 ⅓ cups stoneground wholemeal flour

½ tsp easy-blend dried yeast

1 tbsp caster (superfine) sugar

1 tsp fine sea salt

1 tbsp olive oil

Index